CoreOS in Action

CoreOS in Action

RUNNING APPLICATIONS ON CONTAINER LINUX

MATT BAILEY

MANNING

SHELTER ISLAND

For online information and ordering of this and other Manning books, please visit www.manning.com. The publisher offers discounts on this book when ordered in quantity. For more information, please contact

    Special Sales Department
    Manning Publications Co.
    20 Baldwin Road
    PO Box 761
    Shelter Island, NY 11964
    Email: orders@manning.com

Manning Publications Co.
20 Baldwin Road
PO Box 761
Shelter Island, NY 11964

Development editor:	Cynthia Kane
Review editor:	Ivan Martinović
Project editor:	Tiffany Taylor
Copyeditor:	Tiffany Taylor
Proofreader:	Katie Tennant
Technical proofreader:	Ivan Kirkpatrik
Typesetter:	Dottie Marsico
Cover designer:	Marija Tudor

ISBN 9781617293740
Printed in the United States of America
1 2 3 4 5 6 7 8 9 10 – EBM – 22 21 20 19 18 17

This book is dedicated to my wife, Jenn; and my kids, Adam and Melanie.
Without your gracious absence, I wouldn't have been able to
substitute sleepless nights of diaper changing
for sleepless nights of book writing.

brief contents

contents

acknowledgments

I would like to thank Manning Publications for reaching out to me to start writing this book; and express my thanks to publisher Marjan Bace, to Cynthia Kane for guiding me through this long process, to Ivan Kirkpatrick for his very detailed effort in the technical review of this book, to Tiffany Taylor for helping push the last bits over the line, and to everyone on the editorial and production teams, including Janet Vail, Katie Tennant, Dottie Marsico, and many others who worked behind the scenes. In addition, I'd like to thank all my friends in #gh and #omgp (you know who you are) for always providing encouragement.

I can't thank enough the amazing group of technical peer reviewers, led by Ivan Martinović—Michael Bright, Raffaello Cimbro, Luke Greenleaf, Mike Haller, Sriram Macharla, Palak Mathur, Javier Muñoz Mellid, Thomas Peklak, Austin Riendeau, Kent Spillner, Antonis Tsaltas, Filippo Veneri, and Marco Zuppone—and the talented forum contributors. Their contributions included catching technical mistakes, errors in terminology, and typos, and making topic suggestions. Each pass through the review process and each piece of feedback implemented through the forum topics shaped and molded the manuscript.

preface

As is probably true for many of you reading this book, I started out in the technology industry as a systems administrator for Linux and UNIX systems and networks. Also, like many, I was never satisfied with the levels of (and confidence in) automation available to me. Some of us worked with things like CFEngine, Puppet, and Chef, to manage more with less and to do more serious engineering and less "systems janitoring" with our technology. Then containers became popular, and CoreOS was launched to bridge the gap between containers and systems administration at scale.

I began using CoreOS in late 2013 when it was just getting started. It was the OS that most systems admins knew had to exist eventually: an integrated way to orchestrate services as an abstraction from the pool of compute resources they run on. Manning reached out to me in late 2015 to see if I was interested in writing a CoreOS book, and I pulled together a proposal and started writing. I also began to feel guilty doing anything *other* than writing when I had spare time without my kids around. This is my first book, and I've discovered that coming up with the content and typing it in Vim isn't the hardest part: it's finding the magic alignment of motivated book-writing time and uninterrupted free time. These things rarely happen at once, especially when you have young kids.

I hope this book informs and challenges you. The progression of this book, in a way, follows the progression of my career and the progression of this slice of technology. Specifically, CoreOS and systems like it are intended to turn mundane operations work into software development, and to turn sysadmin firefighting into declarative engineering. So, this book begins with nuts and bolts, and ends with a complete software stack.

about this book

This book serves as a resource for application architects, systems administrators, and anyone seeking information on how to do computing at a large scale without sacrificing development workflow or operational simplicity. CoreOS and its suite of components provide a solid approach to systems design in which high availability, service discovery, and fault tolerance become less painful to implement and are part of your core infrastructure and application architecture from the beginning. CoreOS and the concepts it espouses are useful to both developers and operations professionals; CoreOS realizes the intents of containerization in a way that becomes much easier to operationalize, maintain, and iterate.

If you're reading this book, you've probably noticed a general movement in technology to break down silos and bring together the worlds of development and operations. In many organizations, the roles of operations professionals and application architects are being combined in a role such as DevOps or Site Reliability Engineering. As a result, some people may end up with knowledge gaps. At times, this book may seem to mix information that's obvious to you with more-advanced topics, but that's because I've tried to provide a complete picture for people who may be missing parts of the foundational knowledge required to be successful with CoreOS.

Who should read this book

This book is intended for systems administrators, software engineers, and everyone in between. The book goes into both the operationalization and software architecture of building services using CoreOS; if you're someone who has any interest in building scalable, fault-tolerant systems, this book is for you.

There isn't a lot of functional code in this book—mostly, I show you configuration files and some YAML templates for Amazon Web Services. A basic understanding of Bash and general Linux system administration should be enough to get you started. Later in the book, there are examples of a Node.js service with a JavaScript front end, but JavaScript experience isn't required.

Before I describe the book's chapters, let's look at some technological background and history that led to the creation of CoreOS.

Background

Since around 2008, the need to scale out systems to meet the needs of an organization's customers or manage the load of its own internal compute resources has spawned an entire industry of services, tooling, and consultancies to achieve these scale goals with varying amounts of ease. The ultimate goal was always to manage more scale with less resources—and to do so quickly. These platform-as-a-service (PaaS), infrastructure-as-a-service (IaaS), and configuration-management suites were all designed to shift the burden of systems administration into automated systems so that organizations could "easily" decouple IT manpower from scaling goals. The ideal was captured in a metaphor (which should be attributed to Bill Baker, as best I can find) that you should treat your infrastructure like cattle, not like pets. That is, your unit of computing resource is a commodity or an appliance, not a discrete, well-groomed server with a name. You dispose of cattle if they get sick; you nurse pets back to health. You should make the most of automation, and you shouldn't care too much if you have to rebuild things; doing so should be easy and repeatable.

But the reality of attempting to achieve these goals of repeatability and ephemerality is often exceedingly complex. Your particular way of doing it can become a black box of siloed logic and workflow, even if you're using widely used tools. Configuration-management systems like Chef and Puppet are particularly vulnerable to this complexity—not because they were designed to be, but because organizations often run into obstacles (technical and nontechnical) that end up being solved in ways that are orthogonal to the best practices for these tools. In the IaaS world, organizations often treat their public cloud compute resources just like they treated their on-site resources, mostly because IaaS has the flexibility to allow this, even if it leads to unmaintainable systems. Enter containers.

Containers

LXC was an early effort to create a virtual runtime within the user space of Linux. It was a heavier abstraction than chroots and jails, but a lighter abstraction than full virtualization. Few people used or heard of LXC until Docker started up in 2013 and added a lot of features around LXC's technology, eventually entirely replacing LXC's components with its own. In my opinion, Docker, and containerization in general, solves the problems that virtualization was supposed to: simple isolation of concerns, replication of systems, and immutable runtime state. The benefits are obvious: dependency management becomes easily contained; runtime is standardized; and the approach is developer-friendly enough that development and operations can use the same tools and, byte for byte, the same container. Thus, "It works for me, but not in production" is uttered far fewer times. CoreOS is the operationalization of this computing model in a way that uses the advantages of containerization in a generic, distributed system model.

Throughout this book, you'll learn how to take advantage of this computing model. You'll learn how to deploy and manage CoreOS both in a prototype environment and in production in the cloud. You'll also learn how to design and adapt your application stacks to operate well in this context. In addition to the OS, I'll cover each of CoreOS's components in detail, along with their application: etcd for configuration and discovery, rkt for a different approach to the container runtime, fleet for distributed service scheduling, and flannel for network abstraction.

Distributed computing is nothing new; many models and software packages for distributed systems have been around since the dawn of computing. But most of these systems have been historically obscure, highly proprietary, or cloistered in particular industries like scientific computing. Some of the oldest designs exist today only to support legacy systems from the 1970s that powered distributed computing for mainframes and minicomputers.

History and motivations behind CoreOS

The concept of *single system image* (SSI) computing is an OS architecture that hasn't seen much activity since the 1990s, except for a few cases that have longstanding support to run legacy systems. SSI is an architecture that presents many computers in a cluster as a single system. There is a single filesystem, shared interprocess communication (IPC) via shared runtime space, and process checkpointing/migration. MOSIX/openMosix, Kerrighed, VMScluster, and Plan 9 (natively supported) are all SSI systems. Plan 9 has probably received the most current development activity, which should tell you something about the popularity of this computing model.

The main drawbacks of SSI are, first, that the systems are often extremely difficult to configure and maintain and aren't geared toward generic use. Second, the field has stagnated significantly: there's nothing new in SSI, and it has failed to catch on as a popular model. I think this is because scientific and other Big Data computing have embraced grid-compute, batch operating models like Condor, BOINC, and Slurm. These tools are designed to run compute jobs in a cluster and deliver a result; SSI's shared IPC provides little benefit for these applications, because the cost (in time) of data transmission is eclipsed by the cost of the blocking batch process. In the world of application server stacks, abstractions by protocols like HTTP and distributed queues have also made shared IPC not worth investing in.

The problem space now for distributed computing is how to effectively manage large-scale systems. Whether you're working on a web stack or distributed batch processing, you may not need shared IPC, but the other things that came with SSI have more apparent value: a shared filesystem means you configure only *one* system, and process checkpointing and migration mean nodes are disposable and more "cattle-like." Without shared IPC, these solutions can be difficult to implement. Some organizations turn to configuration-management systems that apply configuration to many machines, or set up extremely complicated monitoring systems full of custom logic. In my experience, configuration-management systems fall short of the goal by only ensuring any state exactly at runtime; after they've made their pass, the state becomes unknown. These systems are more focused on repeatability than consistency, which is a fine goal but doesn't provide the reliability of a shared configuration via a distributed filesystem. Monitoring systems that attempt to also manage processes are often either application-specific or hairy to implement and maintain.

Intentionally or not, container systems like Docker laid the groundwork for resurrecting the advantages of SSI without having to implement shared IPC. Docker guarantees runtime state and provides an execution model that's abstracted from the OS. "But Matt," you may think, "this is the complete opposite of SSI. Every discrete system now has an even more isolated configuration and runtime, not shared!" Yes, this approach is orthogonal, but it achieves the same goals. If runtime state is defined only once (in the Dockerfile, for example) and maintained throughout the life of the container, you've reached the goal of a single point of configuration. And if you can orchestrate the discrete process state both remotely and independently from the OS and the cluster node it's running on, you've achieved the goal of cluster-wide process scheduling of generic services.

Realizing those possibilities is where there needs to be tooling independent of the containerization system. This is where CoreOS and its suite of systems come in. CoreOS provides just enough OS to run a few services; the rest is handled by the orchestration efforts of etcd and fleet—etcd provides a distributed configuration from which containers can define their runtime characteristics, and fleet manages distributed initialization and scheduling of containers. Internally, CoreOS also uses etcd to provide a distributed lock to automatically manage OS upgrades, which in turn uses fleet to balance services across the cluster so that a node can upgrade itself.

This book's roadmap

Chapter 1 starts you off with a brief introduction to the CoreOS ecosystem. I offer some explanation of the core systems in the container OS and a brief example that isn't really designed for you to execute, but rather to illustrate how the parts fit together.

Chapter 2 walks you through the process of setting up a local CoreOS environment that you'll use throughout most of the rest of the book as your sandbox. This is also the process people use in the real world to build things for CoreOS, so it's a good idea to pay close attention to this chapter.

Chapter 3 teaches you about CoreOS's approach to fault tolerance and system upgrades, and will walk you through setting up a fault-tolerant web application. You'll build on this "Hello World" example in the remainder of the book.

Chapter 4 discusses real-world requirements and targets for a production deployment of CoreOS, as well as a real-world example of how to deal with the option of distributed filesystems in a cluster.

Chapter 5 goes into the twelve-factor app methodology and how to apply it to application stacks that you want to deploy in CoreOS. The chapter ends with a preview of how you'll apply this methodology in chapter 6.

Chapter 6 extends the example from chapter 3 into a more realistic web application with many layers. You'll also be introduced to a persistent database layer.

Chapter 7 takes the persistence layer from chapter 6 and dives deep into how to make it fault tolerant and scalable across an entire cluster of machines.

Chapter 8 takes a dive into practical deployment of CoreOS into Amazon Web Services (AWS).

Chapter 9 teaches you how to take the entire software stack you built in chapters 6 and 7 and deploy it with automation into the AWS environment you constructed in chapter 8.

Chapter 10 wraps up the book by discussing the system administration portion of CoreOS, including logging, backups, scaling, and CoreOS's new rkt container system.

Downloading the code

The code for all the examples in this book, including some of the very long AWS templates, is available at www.manning.com/books/coreos-in-action.

About the author

Matt Bailey is currently a technical lead at ZeniMax. He has worked in higher education and with scientific computing, medical, and networking technology companies, as well as a few startups. You can find him online via http://mdb.io.

Author Online

Purchase of *CoreOS in Action* includes free access to a private web forum run by Manning Publications where you can make comments about the book, ask technical questions, and receive help from the author and from other users. To access the forum and subscribe to it, point your web browser to www.manning.com/books/coreos-in-action. This page provides information on how to get on the forum once you're registered, what kind of help is available, and the rules of conduct on the forum.

Manning's commitment to our readers is to provide a venue where a meaningful dialogue between individual readers and between readers and the author can take place. It is not a commitment to any specific amount of participation on the part of the author, whose contribution to Author Online remains voluntary (and unpaid). We suggest you try asking the author some challenging questions lest his interest stray!

The Author Online forum and the archives of previous discussions will be accessible from the publisher's website as long as the book is in print.

About the cover

The figure on the cover of *CoreOS in Action* is a "Dervish of Syria." Muslim dervishes lived in religious communities, much like Christian monks, withdrawing from the world and leading lives of poverty and contemplation; they were known as a source of wisdom, medicine, poetry, enlightenment, and witticisms. The illustration is taken from a collection of costumes of the Ottoman Empire published on January 1, 1802, by William Miller of Old Bond Street, London. The title page is missing from the collection, and we have been unable to track it down to date. The book's table of contents identifies the figures in both English and French, and each illustration bears the names of two artists who worked on it, both of whom would no doubt be surprised to find their art gracing the front cover of a computer programming book … 200 years later.

Dress codes have changed since then, and the diversity by region, so rich at the time, has faded away. It's now often hard to tell the inhabitant of one continent from another. Perhaps, trying to view it optimistically, we have traded a cultural and visual diversity for a more varied personal life—or a more varied and interesting intellectual and technical life. We at Manning celebrate the inventiveness, the initiative, and, yes, the fun of the computer business with book covers based on the rich diversity of regional life of two centuries ago, brought back to life by the pictures from this collection.

Part 1

Getting to know CoreOS

In these first three chapters, you'll get to know what CoreOS is all about. I'll cover some terminology and the systems that form CoreOS and get you up and running with a sandbox environment. You'll also start working on an application stack that you'll build on throughout the book.

Introduction to the CoreOS family

This chapter covers

- Overview of CoreOS systems and concepts
- Understanding common workflow patterns for CoreOS
- Introducing fleet and etcd, and systemd units

Suppose you've been hired by a new company that wants you to build out a modern infrastructure and operational architecture for its developers. The company has a wide range of application stacks, and you have strong requirements around horizontal scalability and high availability. You know you want Linux, but the idea of maintaining endless operating system updates and changes or setting up complex configuration-management systems is unappealing. You recognize that containerization can make this far easier—you can separate the operational configuration from the applications'—but you're still left with how to manage all those containers at scale. Plenty of distributions today support Docker, but not in a way that seems designed for large-scale production use.

Enter CoreOS: an OS designed from the ground up to facilitate container operationalization at any scale. It's highly fault tolerant and extremely lightweight, and it
appears performant, but how do you get started? You know the goal: you want to provide your engineers with a container-based platform as a service, and you know
CoreOS can be the hammer to hit that nail. But how do you get it running? How do
you adapt or design application architectures to best take advantage of this system?

> **NOTE**   If you want to know more about where the ideas in CoreOS came
> from, be sure to read the "Background" section in the "About this book" por-
> tion of this book's front matter.

In this chapter, we'll go over the various parts that make up the CoreOS family of systems, and we'll look a little at how they can solve infrastructure and architecture problems like those just described. By the end of this chapter, you'll have a clear
understanding of CoreOS and how its core components fit together, along with some
ideas about its utility that you can take into chapter 2, when we discuss building out a
local cluster.

1.1   *Meet CoreOS*

CoreOS is here to solve your scale, availability, and deployment workflow problems. In
this chapter, we'll go through a simple application deployment of NGINX (a popular
HTTP server) to illustrate how CoreOS achieves some of these solutions, and review
some essential systems. With CoreOS, you won't have to manage packages, initiate
lengthy upgrade processes, plan out complex configuration files, fiddle with permissions, plan significant maintenance windows (for the OS), or deal with complicated
configuration schema changes. If you fully embrace CoreOS's features, your cluster of
nodes will always have the latest version of the OS, and you won't have any downtime.

These ideas can be a little difficult to grasp when you're first getting started with
CoreOS, but they embody the philosophy of an immutable OS after boot, which creates an experience with the OS that you probably aren't used to. CoreOS's distributed
scheduler, *fleet*, manages the state of your application stack, and CoreOS provides the
platform on which those systems orchestrate your services. If you have a computer sci-
ence background, you can consider traditional configuration-management systems as
relying heavily on *side effects* to constantly manipulate the state of the OS, whereas in
CoreOS, the state of the OS is created once on boot, never changes, and is lost on
shutdown. This is a powerful concept, and it forces architectures with high degrees of
idempotence and no hidden side effects, the results of which are vastly improved certainty about the reliability of your systems and drastically reduced need for layers of
complex tooling to monitor and manage OSs. In this section, I provide an overview of
the parts that make CoreOS tick and how they complement each other.

CoreOS background

CoreOS is a Linux distribution based, in a way, on Gentoo Linux. Similar to how Google's Chrome OS is based on Gentoo, this only matters for those interested in hacking on CoreOS itself, which isn't covered in this book (although this book would certainly be an excellent guide to understanding what you're working on).

The reason this probably doesn't matter to you is a bit more complicated. CoreOS is designed to present a small number of services that act as a lightweight, distributed system; the point of CoreOS is that it mostly stays out of your way, and it's immutably configured on boot, much as a container is. This is very different from virtually all other Linux distributions or OSs as a whole. In chapter 8, we'll dive deeper into cloud-config, which describes the state of the OS, most of which is concerned with cluster discovery and initializing core services that you may want to manage outside of fleet.

On containerization

We'll go into how you can tune your containers to best function with CoreOS, but you should have some experience with Docker and the concepts of containerization to get the most out of this book. You can also check out *Docker in Action* by Jeff Nickoloff (Manning, 2016, www.manning.com/books/docker-in-action).

1.1.1 The CoreOS family

CoreOS consists of a few critical systems and services that manage all the scalability and fault tolerance it claims to facilitate. Figure 1.1 provides a high-level idea of how the cluster layout looks.

We'll go into each of these components in some detail in the next section, and significantly more detail later in the book, but this represents the key systems that make up CoreOS:

- *etcd* acts as your cluster's persistent configuration state (see section 1.1.2).
- *fleetd* acts as your cluster's distributed runtime scheduler (see section 1.1.3).
- *systemd* unit files are the mechanism by which fleetd executes the runtime (see section 1.1.4).
- *Docker and rkt* are the common container platforms that your unit files will run. CoreOS intends all of your runtime to happen in containers, and you can choose from these two platforms (or a combination of both; see section 1.1.5).

The one essential system missing from figure 1.1 is *cloud-config*, which is used to set the initial configuration state of a machine. It's more a detail of infrastructure configuration than a requirement to understand CoreOS's concepts; section 1.1.6 covers it in detail.

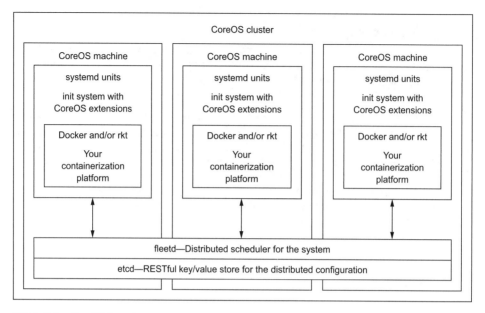

Figure 1.1 CoreOS layout

1.1.2 *etcd and the distributed configuration state*

etcd is a high-reliability distributed key/value store. If you're familiar with memcached or redis, it's similar, but with more focus on (distributed) consistency and availability over performance. It's accessible via custom command-line tools and is fully RESTful and JSON based. As its name implies, etcd is designed to distribute your system and services configuration. It's the data store for fleet (CoreOS's distributed scheduler).

fleet and CoreOS use etcd to find peers, distribute locks for various purposes, and orchestrate running systemd units across the cluster. Although it's useful in that regard alone, it's also designed to be your place to persist configuration in the cluster. In the example later in this chapter, you'll use it to register NGINX instances for a load balancer to discover.

etcd isn't designed for large-object storage or massive performance; its primary purpose is to make the state of the cluster singular. Beyond cloud-config, which sets initial state, no other state (that isn't ephemeral) exists on any particular CoreOS node. etcd provides a way to have state be a property of the compute cluster as a whole and not of any discrete node. It also provides a common bus around which to design more advanced features that take advantage of the single-system nature of the cluster.

You can manipulate etcd with either its own CLI tool, `etcdctl`, or with any HTTP client like `curl`, although the latter usually requires a lot more verbosity—the trade-off for its ubiquity. We'll go into more advanced usage and configuration of etcd later in the book.

1.1.3 *fleet and the distributed service state*

fleet is the other side of the coin from etcd. It enables CoreOS to act as a single machine by distributing systemd units intelligently across your CoreOS cluster, using etcd to distribute this state. Across the cluster, you can easily tell fleet to start up any number of service units, and it will distribute what you've requested either evenly across the cluster or based on some extended configuration of your unit files, which we'll discuss briefly later in this chapter.

This is where the advantages of CoreOS begin to emerge. You can take advantage of the size of your CoreOS cluster for both capacity and high availability with fleet and start to use your entire deployment as a single pool of resources. We'll go into further detail about fleet and how it interacts with unit files throughout the book.

1.1.4 *systemd as CoreOS's init system*

systemd is a relatively new init system designed to tackle significantly more features than the traditional sysvinit system. It's a bit maligned by many users who think it does too much or is counter to how they think an init system should be designed. Nevertheless, it has gained significant momentum—enough that most Linux distributions have switched or will switch entirely to systemd.

CoreOS uses systemd extensively, and you'll need to understand and write systemd unit files to run services in CoreOS. There is, of course, a lot of documentation out there on how to use systemd. I won't go into great detail in this book but will focus on what you need to know about systemd and unit files to be effective in CoreOS. You'll also learn how to use fleet's extensions to systemd to give your units awareness of the cluster; and you'll learn how fleet interacts with the systemd journal, which is critical to understanding how logging works in CoreOS.

1.1.5 *Docker and/or rkt, your container runtimes*

Docker and rkt are the supported runtimes in CoreOS for your services. rkt is a newer container system developed by the CoreOS folks.

First, for clarity, CoreOS supports both Docker and rkt runtime environments; rkt can run Docker containers as well, right alongside the App Container (appc) specification images (ACIs) it was built to support. rkt was built to have more robust privilege separation and to integrate more easily with Linux init systems. It has no daemon like Docker does, and it relies on whatever init system you use to manage process control for a container. This is, of course, systemd in CoreOS, but rkt can be run anywhere.

Whether you choose rkt or Docker (or both) for abstracting your runtimes, what you gain from these container systems is fully realized in CoreOS. The ephemeral nature of container runtimes becomes the way in which you abstract state from the cluster as a whole, as long as you're mindful to follow best practices of constructing containerized architectures in general. We'll cover application architecture in CoreOS in far more depth later in the book.

Brief history of container-like systems

Although container systems like Docker have recently become extremely popular (no doubt due to the vastly improved tooling versus other implementations), containerization isn't particularly new. Docker originally depended on LXC, and systems like chroot jails, FreeBSD jail, Solaris Zones, and others have been around for quite a while to try to solve these same problems. The goal is an abstracted runtime that doesn't require a full virtual machine hardware abstraction, which usually has a high overhead and operational cost.

In my opinion, Docker has been successful because of the high-quality suite of tooling it brings with it and the community that has grown around the product. It's also relatively easy to get up and running with Docker, which certainly can't be said for the other systems mentioned.

1.1.6   *Initial configuration with cloud-config*

Much of the OS configuration of CoreOS is not meant to be manipulated unless you're debugging the OS itself for development. The scope of configuration for CoreOS is entirely contained within the cloud-config file.

Confusingly, the CoreOS folks named this system similarly to the system it's inspired by: *cloud-init*, which is a widely used, YAML-based, initial configuration system. cloud-init isn't unique to CoreOS; you'll see it everywhere if you've had experience using Ubuntu or CentOS in AWS or OpenStack. Developers often use cloud-init to bootstrap other, heavier configuration-management systems like Chef and Puppet, but CoreOS intends cloud-config to be the single source of truth for the OS configuration. It would be possible to use cloud-config to bootstrap systems like Chef, but doing so would be antithetical to the intentions of CoreOS nodes to be single-state and ephemeral.

The minimal cloud-config file usually consists of a discovery token and some SSH keys.

Why cloud-config vs. traditional configuration management?

The benefit of CoreOS building cloud-config is that it's well tailored to fit the needs of initial configuration in the context of how CoreOS approaches OS design. Rather than learning filesystem layouts and nuances about how a distribution splits and manages configuration files, you interface with the base configuration with a configuration abstraction that's easy to use.

CoreOS is designed from the ground up to not have any configuration requirements beyond what you can define in cloud-config, so other systems to do this are unnecessary. For example, you can define new service units by enumerating them in a YAML list, and cloud-config will handle the rest.

1.2   *Fitting together the core services*

Now that you have an understanding of the essential systems that make CoreOS function, we'll look at how they operate with each other to orchestrate running a high-availability service. We'll start with the workflow you're likely to encounter in your day-to-day operations and walk through the steps of setting up an example NGINX HTTP server in a cluster.

Orchestration of your application stacks is where CoreOS and its tools bring you a lot of power and flexibility. But you need to learn how the instruments work before you can compose sophisticated systems.

1.2.1   *The CoreOS workflow*

The workflow for setting up a basic cluster of NGINX instances looks like the flow in figure 1.2. It's best if you consider CoreOS and its systems to be the manifestation of container ideals in operations and infrastructure. Embrace ephemerality, and forget notions about how you've managed servers in the past; most of them don't apply. Think of the cluster as a single mechanism to achieve your goals, not a group of devices that need meticulous management. Once you're in this mindset, the scaling vectors will be obvious and the opportunities for fault tolerance will be easily accomplished.

Figure 1.2 represents a basic workflow: you create the Docker or rkt containers and systemd units to support your NGINX server, submit your units to the cluster with fleet, and, based on any options specified in your unit file (or the absence of options), fleet will decide on which machine your service should run. fleet has two main concerns: *machines*, which are CoreOS nodes (actual physical servers or virtual machines) in the cluster, and *units*, which are the systemd service units it manages. Specifically, units are the plain-text configuration for systemd services; fleet adds context around them and distributes them via etcd. I'll use these terms consistently throughout the rest of the book. There's a lot of detail missing here, of course, but this is the day-to-day workflow of making things happen on your CoreOS cluster.

Many of the benefits you get from CoreOS are achieved from this pattern of deployment. You can submit your unit to any machine in the fleet—they all do exactly the same thing. If a machine becomes unreachable, fleet will run NGINX on a different machine. If you want at least two instances of NGINX running, fleet will distribute them appropriately based on your parameters. fleet is the glue that holds the runtime of your services together across the cluster and makes CoreOS the cluster-aware system it is.

"But what about the rest?" you may ask. Distributing a process or processes across a cluster isn't the entire story, and we'll go into more detail in the next section with a brief example. What you should take away from this is the following: assuming that your CoreOS cluster is set up and running (as discussed in chapter 2) and that your NGINX server is already containerized, making a fault-tolerant, scalable environment with your service is relatively simple.

As your application stack increases in complexity, these goals become more complex in implementation; but they still follow this basic pattern, which is generic

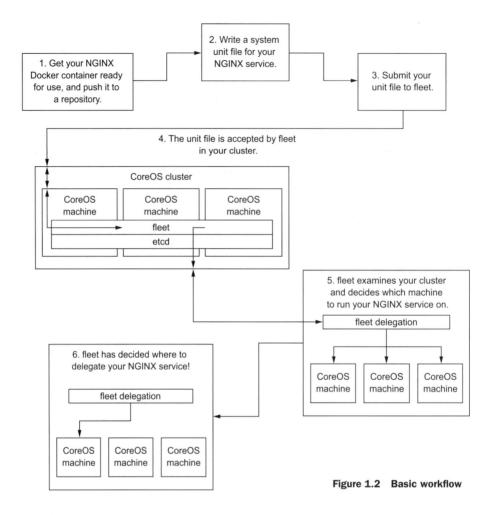

Figure 1.2   Basic workflow

enough to work with many possible architectures. We'll look at more-complex examples beginning in chapter 3.

1.2.2 Creating and running services

This example assumes that you're tasked with getting a website up and running on NGINX with a high degree of fault tolerance and availability. You'll see some far more complete beginning-to-end examples later in this book, but this first taste of how CoreOS functions should give you an idea of the route you'll take to success in your own applications as well as the practical examples and scenarios presented in the book.

> **NOTE**   This is just a warm-up and isn't intended to be an example that you build out. We won't cover setting up the development environment until chapter 2; so, if you're reading the book in order, you won't have a place to run it anyway.

As a read-along example, this is intended to provide familiar terms and concepts so that you have a basic understanding of how systemd, fleet, etcd, and Docker work together in concert in a CoreOS cluster before the practical examples begin. It assumes some things that you probably don't have: a Docker container built with your NGINX config, and a configured CoreOS cluster.

First, you'll get acquainted with the common infrastructure topology of your cluster, shown in figure 1.3. This imagined infrastructure consists of three CoreOS machines and a load balancer. We'll assume that the load balancer is capable of polling a RESTful API for configuration, which will become important later when we go into how services are discovered in your cluster with etcd.

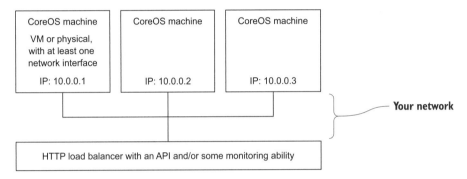

Figure 1.3   Example cluster

1.2.3   *Creating your unit files*

fleet uses systemd as its init system to manage and distribute services; systemd also acts as fleet's entry point for gathering state and manipulating services. systemd is relatively new, but as you may know, it's becoming more of a standard across most popular Linux distributions. If you aren't familiar with systemd unit files, don't worry; there isn't much complexity to what you have to know about unit files to be effective in CoreOS, and you'll learn progressively more about them throughout the book.

You now need to write a couple of systemd unit-file templates: one for NGINX and one for a *sidekick*. A sidekick service is a systemd unit that's tied to your actual service and that performs various actions based on the state of the service. Sidekick services are primarily used for service discovery so that internal and external systems can understand the state of your services. Sidekick units aren't always required, but if something will eventually rely on the announcement or discovery of a service—in this case, your load balancer—you'll need one to take care of that transaction.

First, here's an NGINX template unit that you might use to run your server container.

Listing 1.1 NGINX unit file: nginx@.service

```
[Unit]
Description=My Nginx Server - %i
Requires=docker.service
After=docker.service
```

Ensures that the service only runs after Docker has started, which is important for reboot scenarios

```
[Service]
ExecStartPre=-/usr/bin/docker kill nginx-%i
ExecStartPre=-/usr/bin/docker rm nginx-%i
ExecStartPre=/usr/bin/docker pull my/nginx:latest
ExecStart=/usr/bin/docker run --name mynginx-%i -p 80:80 my/nginx:latest
```

Unit-file options specifically for fleet

```
[X-Fleet]
Conflicts=nginx@*.service
```

Conflicts ensures that only one instance of **NGINX** will run on a single machine. It's rare that you'd want two of the same service on one machine, because the load would be unpredictable. The * means this service will conflict with any template argument between the @ and .service.

Such a unit file is called a *template* because it has an @ in the filename; it's not runnable directly, but anything you add after the @ and before .service is inserted into the unit file wherever `%i` appears. For example, if your unit file is named nginx@.service and you start your service with a command like `fleetctl start nginx@1.service`, `fleetctl` will know to use that file and to replace any `%i` in the file with 1. More on the mechanics later, but this is how you scale your services with multiple instances of the same service.

Next, you need to write an nginx-sidekick template.

Listing 1.2 nginx-sidekick unit file: nginx-sidekick@.service

Means the sidekick will become dependent on the **NGINX** service matching the same %i. This dependency will function only if it's running on the same machine (see the last line of this listing).

```
[Unit]
Description=Register Nginx - %i
BindsTo=nginx@%i.service
After=nginx@%i.service

[Service]
ExecStart=/bin/sh -c "while true; \
  do etcdctl set /services/www/nginx@%i \
  '{ \"host\": \"%H\", \"port\": 80 }' --ttl 60;sleep 45; \
  done"
ExecStop=/usr/bin/etcdctl rm /services/www/nginx@%i

[X-Fleet]
MachineOf=nginx@%i.service
```

Removes the key on stop. It will automatically be removed if this is never executed (for example, due to a power failure).

Binds the sidekick to the same machine as its partner **NGINX** service

Writes a **JSON** object to the etcd cluster every 45 seconds with a time to live of 60 seconds. As long as the partner **NGINX** service is running, the sidekick will continue to write configuration information to etcd.

Now, your systemd unit files are ready, and you can register them with `fleetctl` from your workstation:

```
$ fleetctl --tunnel=10.0.0.1 start nginx@1.service nginx-sidekick@1.service
```

You can choose any of your nodes to `--tunnel` to, and `fleetctl` will automatically upload the unit files to the cluster (via SSH) and start them on one of your nodes. Notice that I put the numeral 1 after the @; `fleetctl` is smart enough to know this means it's a systemd template and will grab the correct file.

If you want to upload your services and not start them, you can replace `start` with `submit`. We'll go into greater detail about fleet and `fleetctl` in chapters 2 and 3.

Your service is now up and running, and your load balancer should have picked up where NGINX is running based on watching etcd. You can check the status of your running services with `fleetctl` as well:

```
$ fleetctl --tunnel=10.0.0.1 list-units
UNIT                        MACHINE              ACTIVE   SUB
nginx-sidekick@1.service    22f78fd4.../10.0.0.1 active   running
nginx@1.service             22f78fd4.../10.0.0.1 active   running
```

You may see the status as `inactive` for the sidekick and `activating` for NGINX. What's happening is that Docker is downloading the image layers for the first time, so it could take a few minutes to get both in an active/running state. Because the sidekick is tied to the service, it won't run until the service is properly started.

You can also check to see whether the sidekick server has registered your NGINX server:

```
$ etcdctl get /services/www/nginx@1        ◁──  We'll dive into etcd a little more in chapters 2
{ "host": "core-01", "port": 80 }                and 3; this is more or less just an HTTP request.
```

Now that your service and sidekick are up and running, let's look at how failover works.

1.2.4 *Service topology and failover*

The state of your service (nginx@1) and sidekick (nginx-sidekick@1) in your cluster now looks something like figure 1.4. As mentioned, you assume that the load balancer can poll etcd by hitting etcd for /services/www/nginx@1 and using the JSON response to set its own configuration.

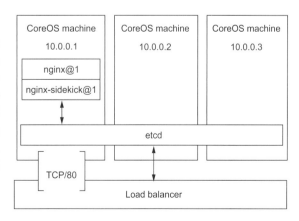

Figure 1.4   Cluster with services running

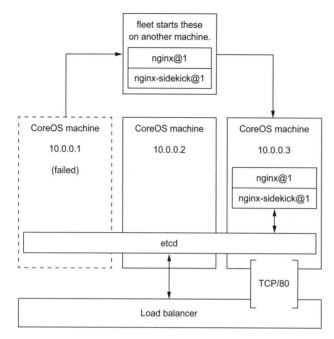

Figure 1.5   Someone owes you doughnuts.

Let's test the level of fault tolerance. Say the new intern trips in the data center and knocks the network cable out of your 10.0.0.1 machine. Once fleet realizes that the machine is gone, figure 1.5 shows what will happen.

Let's go through this machine failure step by step:

1   fleet finds out via etcd that 10.0.0.1 is gone.
2   fleet knows from records in etcd that nginx@1 and its sidekick nginx-sidekick@1 were running on that machine.
3   fleet starts up nginx@1 on 10.0.0.3, and nginx-sidekick@1 follows.
4   nginx-sidekick@1 updates information in etcd about what host nginx@1 is now running on.
5   Your load balancer, which is polling all etcd endpoints, reconfigures itself based on new etcd information.

With everything configured properly, you have a solid failover solution; but that's not so great on its own. Simple failover certainly isn't *highly available*—you still have an outage. What do you need? More services!

A good systems architect knows not to confuse *capacity scaling* with *availability scaling*: in reality, they may be conflated, but you should never rely on that conflation. These concepts are fleshed out in CoreOS, as well. Adding more services of the same type does, indeed, increase capacity, but the goal might be to improve high availability (HA). When you do your planning, remember to pay attention to your failure points and consider them an availability multiplier for your capacity. We'll go into capacity and availability planning starting in chapter 4.

How do you get more services going? You're in luck: you already planned for this by making systemd unit templates! Start them with `fleetctl`:

```
$ fleetctl --tunnel=10.0.0.1 start nginx@2.service nginx-sidekick@2.service
```

That's it! Notice that I didn't change the IP address, mostly to illustrate that it doesn't matter which host you tunnel through. The unit file tells fleet that any NGINX service `Conflicts` with any other NGINX service, so the service will automatically run on a different machine.

Your cluster now looks like figure 1.6, and `fleetctl` reports two more services and sidekicks running:

```
$ fleetctl --tunnel=10.0.0.1 list-units
UNIT                          MACHINE                  ACTIVE   SUB
nginx-sidekick@1.service      6c945e2e.../10.0.0.3     active   running
nginx-sidekick@2.service      22f78fd4.../10.0.0.1     active   running
nginx@1.service               6c945e2e.../10.0.0.3     active   running
nginx@2.service               22f78fd4.../10.0.0.1     active   running
```

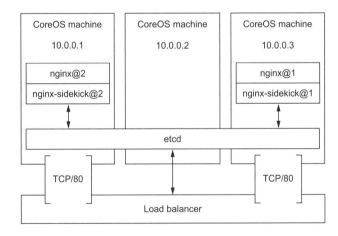

Figure 1.6   Two NGINXs!

If any one of these machines fails, its services will move to another machine in the cluster, as previously described, and you won't have an outage because your load balancer will still have one running service to rely on. If two machines fail, then—best case—you'll be running at half capacity, because you'll have only one NGINX instance running. At the worst, if those two machines are the ones running the two services, you'll have an outage while one of the services starts up on the single remaining machine.

As I said earlier, you'll want to think about what this means for your capacity planning, because you wouldn't want to overload a single instance of NGINX if one failed. CoreOS, of course, supports having far more than three machines; thinking about how to plan out your cluster for failure and capacity is something we'll cover in chapters 4 and 5.

1.3   *Summary*

- The basic components of CoreOS consist of etcd, fleet, systemd, and cloud-config:
  - etcd maintains configuration and discovery state.
  - fleet schedules services across the cluster.
  - systemd is used as an init system.
  - cloud-config sets up the initial immutable state of a machine.
- systemd unit files and optional sidekicks are distributed by fleet to compose high-availability services.
- With the appropriate configurations, fault tolerance can be built into most existing systems.

Getting started
on your workstation

This chapter covers

- Running a Vagrant environment for CoreOS
- Configuring your local development cluster
- Starting to use the CoreOS set of tools

Much like setting up a development environment for writing software, it's common practice to run a CoreOS cluster on your local machine. You'll be able to use this environment to try out various configuration settings, clustering options, and, of course, your unit files before starting them in a real compute cluster. This gives you the ability to work on CoreOS without many dependencies, as well as the ability to completely blow up your systems without impacting anyone else.

You'll use this virtualized local cluster on your machine as a workspace throughout the book and build all the example application stacks using it until the discussion gets to production deployments of CoreOS. This will let you dive into CoreOS in a well-supported way without having to deal with any of the details of normal infrastructure.

17

We'll begin this chapter by looking at how to set up Vagrant, a common virtualization tool, and deploy a CoreOS cluster to it. We'll then explore some of the basic tooling to interact with this workspace. Finally, we'll go through the chapter 1 example of deploying a simple NGINX service to your new cluster and see how to interact with it in the context of CoreOS. By the end of this chapter, you should be set up with a three-node cluster and have a basic understanding of how to administer CoreOS, which will be essential once we dive into more-complex examples later in the book.

2.1 Setting up Vagrant

Vagrant (www.vagrantup.com) is an open source tool from HashiCorp to set up and manage virtual machines for development. It's great for consistent development-environment bootstrapping; it's a tool that acts as a configuration wrapper for a VM hypervisor of your choice. It officially supports VMware and VirtualBox; we'll use VirtualBox (www.virtualbox.org) for all the examples in this book, because it's also open source and freely available.

> **NOTE** This chapter is the only place I'll provide instructions for Windows, OS X, and Linux. After this, for the sake of simplicity, I'll assume you have a UNIX-like OS on your workstation. There are a few more hoops you have to jump through on Windows that I'll address later in this chapter.

Other test environment options (AWS, GCE, and so on)

It's not absolutely required that you run your development environment on your workstation. Some people prefer to keep a development environment in the cloud for mobility reasons, or share a development environment among coworkers, or have a development environment that more closely resembles production. Although those approaches aren't as easy or convenient as using a local cluster, CoreOS offers guides and resources for setting things up on public cloud providers with the least friction possible.

The list of officially supported platforms and how to get started with them is available at https://coreos.com/os/docs/latest/#running-coreos. Keep in mind that we'll explore a complete AWS production deployment later in this book.

> **NOTE** Command-line examples throughout this chapter have two possible locations from which they're run. If the example command starts with host$, it's a command you're running from your workstation; if it starts with core@core-01 ~ $ (where 01 can be any number), it's meant to be run from the CoreOS machine. In section 2.2, you'll see how to use fleetctl with an SSH tunnel; command-line examples later in the book that begin with $ assume you're using this tunnel, in which case it doesn't matter whether you're running the command from your host or on a CoreOS node.

2.1.1   *Requirements and setup*

Ideally, you're running Windows, Linux, or OS X in a 64-bit flavor and on x86. It's probably not impossible to run this on ARM or in 32-bit, but CoreOS only supports x86 on 64-bit, and I don't want to cover the performance and usability impact of using an alternative architecture on the hypervisor host machine. This book's examples will also be a lot easier to work through if you're on anything but Windows, because you can run some of the tools from your local workstation. I haven't tried this with the new Ubuntu for Windows 10 runtime: it may offer an easier environment for Windows users.

You'll also want at least 3 GB of memory available to run your VMs (1 GB for each VM). You can get by with less, but this will be my assumption for the examples. You can either tune the VMs to use less, or accept the performance impact of over-allocating VM memory (meaning your host will start swapping). I also recommend having a four-core CPU, but that's a little less important for this setup. You'll allocate one CPU per VM, but over-allocating here shouldn't have a huge impact. The biggest performance bottleneck will, of course, be I/O; if you can use a solid-state drive for this, it will greatly enhance your experience.

Your first step in getting up and running is to install VirtualBox. You can get the appropriate 64-bit version of VirtualBox from www.virtualbox.org; you may also choose to install the Oracle VM VirtualBox Extension Pack if you meet the requirements of its license, but it isn't required. Alternatively, you can install VirtualBox from whatever package manager you use (APT, Homebrew, and so on). The installation should be straightforward on any OS. You may need to reboot.

Next, you need to install Vagrant. The same procedure applies: grab the installer (64-bit) from www.vagrantup.com, or install it with your OS's package manager. At the time of writing, the latest versions of the VirtualBox and Vagrant packages (VirtualBox 5.0 and Vagrant 1.8) are well beyond the minimum required versions for CoreOS.

You also need Git installed to clone the coreos/coreos-vagrant repository. This should be available (or already installed, in some cases) through your OS's package manager. For Windows, the easiest option—if you're not already conversant with Git and you use some other client—is to install GitHub's desktop client from https://desktop.github.com. You can also use this in OS X, but the command-line Git is provided for you in OS X. You don't need a lot of Git experience; only one command is needed to get you up and running.

You'll also want to grab the code repository for this book. Although most of the code listings (as with most technical books) are best committed to memory by typing them out rather than copying and pasting, there are some *very* long listings in later chapters that you should use from the repo. It's available at www.manning.com/books/coreos-in-action.

2.1.2   *Getting Vagrant up and running*

Now that you've got everything installed, let's look at how things will fit together once you're done with this section (see figure 2.1). Your development cluster will consist of three CoreOS machines (core01–03) running within VirtualBox.

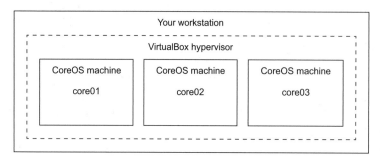

**Figure 2.1
Workstation
configuration**

CLONING THE VAGRANT REPOSITORY

Follow these steps on your workstation:

1   Somewhere in your filesystem, `git clone` CoreOS's Vagrant repository (coreos/coreos-vagrant). Here's the command on OS X or Linux (or Windows command-line only):

```
host$ git clone https://github.com/coreos/coreos-vagrant.git
```

2   In a web browser, navigate to https://github.com/coreos/coreos-vagrant (see figure 2.2). Click Save to Desktop, and the desktop client's clone window will open.

Figure 2.2   Open the repository in GitHub Desktop.

3 Choose a directory to clone the repo to, and click OK (see figure 2.3).

Figure 2.3   Choose a path to save the repository to.

4 If you're in Windows, you'll likely want to change the shell to Git Bash: it will have better terminal compatibility once you get into CoreOS. To do so, open the options for GitHub Desktop (as shown in figure 2.4); then, under Default Shell, select Git Bash, and click Save (see figure 2.5).

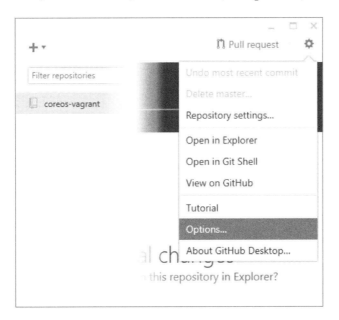

Figure 2.4   Open the GitHub Desktop options.

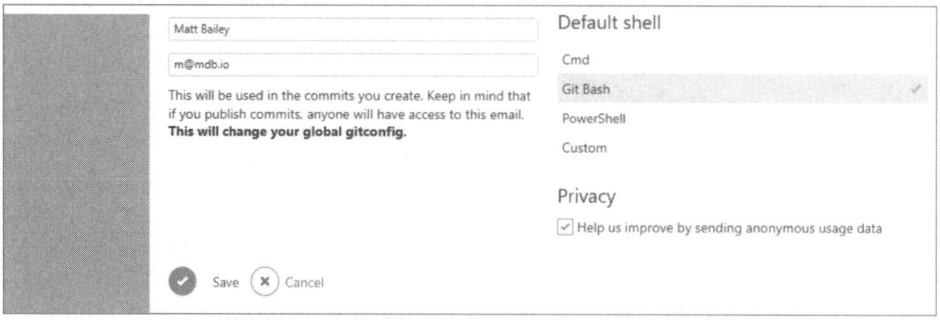

Figure 2.5   Select Git Bash as your default shell.

EDITING VAGRANT'S SETTINGS

Now that everything is downloaded, we can look at how to configure Vagrant for your CoreOS development environment:

1   Make copies of and rename the sample configuration files: copy user-data.sample to just user-data (no extension), and copy and rename config.rb.sample to config.rb.

2   Open config.rb so that you can change a few parameters to get Vagrant up and running properly. On the first few lines, you'll see the following:

```
# Size of the CoreOS cluster created by Vagrant
$num_instances=1
```

To tell Vagrant (via the Vagrantfile configuration file) to start up three CoreOS instances, change the variable to read as follows:

```
# Size of the CoreOS cluster created by Vagrant
$num_instances=3
```

> **Cluster configuration**
>
> All the examples will show the benefits of CoreOS in a cluster configuration, and three machines is the minimum for etcd clustering. If you're resource-constrained on your desktop, you can choose to do only one instance, but understand that you probably won't get a good sense of how CoreOS manages things at scale.
>
> A single instance is fine for development once you're comfortable with the platform, but I highly recommend a cluster configuration to learn all of CoreOS's features.

3   You may also want to tweak some other settings in config.rb. CPU and memory settings can be uncommented and changed near the end of the file:

```
# Customize VMs
#$vm_gui = false
#$vm_memory = 1024
#$vm_cpus = 1
```

You can also share some filesystems across the VM from your host machine. I won't go into this, but it may be useful for Windows users who aren't comfortable using command-line editors to build unit files.

GETTING INTO YOUR SHELL

Next, you open a shell session to interact with Vagrant. If you're using the GitHub Desktop client, right-click the coreos-vagrant repository and click Open in Git Shell (see figure 2.6) so you can interact inside the Git repository. Doing so opens the shell shown in figure 2.7.

Right-click, and choose Open in Git Shell.

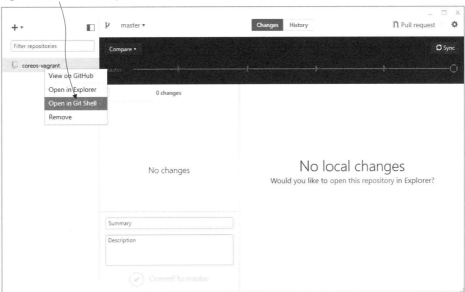

Figure 2.6 Open the Git shell with GitHub Desktop

Figure 2.7 Git Bash shell

At this point, I'm finished with screenshots until I start talking about Amazon Web Services in chapter 8. All the commands are the same across all platforms—Vagrant is great for standardizing these kinds of development environments.

2.1.3 Getting a CoreOS cluster running in Vagrant

You're now ready to start up your cluster. If you had to opt for a single-instance deployment, note that the output will look slightly different, but the commands are the same.

Let's start Vagrant! With the coreos-vagrant repository as your current working directory in your shell, issue this command:

```
host$ vagrant up
```

You'll see a bunch of things happen, which will look something like this:

```
Bringing machine 'core-01' up with 'virtualbox' provider...
Bringing machine 'core-02' up with 'virtualbox' provider...
Bringing machine 'core-03' up with 'virtualbox' provider...
==> core-01: Importing base box 'coreos-alpha'...
...etc
```

Once the operation has completed, you can verify that everything is up and running properly by logging in to one of the machines and using `fleetctl` to check the cluster:

```
host$ vagrant ssh core-01
CoreOS alpha (928.0.0)
core@core-01 ~ $ fleetctl list-machines
MACHINE      IP              METADATA
45b08438... 172.17.8.102    -
cac39fc1... 172.17.8.101    -
cf69ccab... 172.17.8.103    -
```

> Because this is your first time connecting to this node, you may have to accept an SSH host key, which you should be familiar with.

If something didn't work right or was interrupted unexpectedly, you can always run `vagrant destroy` to start over. If you see three machines, you're finished! You now have a local cluster of CoreOS machines.

> **NOTE** It's important to remember that you must remain in the directory where your Vagrantfile is, to interact with your Vagrant machines. Once you change directories in your shell, things like `vagrant ssh` won't work.

2.2 Tooling for interacting with CoreOS

Your Vagrant cluster of CoreOS machines is up and running, and it's time to learn about the tooling that's essential to interact with CoreOS. CoreOS uses the Bash shell, and I'll assume you have some familiarity with it as well as SSH.

This section covers the essential tools to use CoreOS: `fleetctl` and `etcdctl`. We'll also visit the Toolbox, which is useful for debugging anything you might run into in a more familiar Linux administration environment; and we'll go over how CoreOS may appear different than what you're used to if you're an experienced Linux admin.

A note about editors

You should understand that Vim is the only installed editor on CoreOS. Ultimately, your workflow won't involve editing files directly on CoreOS, but for the sake of learning how things work on CoreOS, you'll need *some way* to get systemd unit files on your cluster.

If you absolutely don't want to use Vim, here are a few options:

- As mentioned in the previous section, you can tell Vagrant to mount some directories across from your host machine, and then you can use your favorite editor to write your files (Windows users: be mindful of your line endings).
- CoreOS comes with Git, so you can put your files in a repository and push and pull them to your instances.
- You'll see later in this chapter how to use the CoreOS Toolbox, which allows you to install various software packages in a Docker container that mounts the CoreOS filesystem within it.
- If you're using Linux or OS X, `fleetctl` and `etcdctl` work remotely (over SSH) if you install them on your host machine. We'll go into this in the next section.

While you're learning about the basics of CoreOS, this book will assume you're editing some files directly on the box (with Vim), because that's the most universal option. Obviously, you're going to want to set up a more formal workflow for using CoreOS in production and across a team; we'll go into that later in the book.

`fleetctl` and `etcdctl` will be your most commonly used tools in CoreOS. They aren't especially complicated to use, but you'll want to be well acquainted with how they function to do anything in your CoreOS cluster. A bit of a refresher: fleet is CoreOS's distributed scheduler; it decides when, where, and how your containers run within your cluster. It acts as an orchestrater for systemd and represents service state within your cluster. Together, for example, fleet and systemd decide how many and which machines run an NGINX service. etcd is CoreOS's distributed configuration store; it gives you a consistent place to manage and inspect the configuration state of your cluster. These two systems make CoreOS work, and they're the foundation on which you can take advantage of what CoreOS offers.

Before getting started with the tools, the handiest way to use fleet and etcd is from your host machine, rather than having to `ssh` directly to a CoreOS node before you do anything. But this will only work on OSs that aren't Windows (although I haven't tried it on the new Ubuntu Windows 10 runtime). You can install these with your package manager of choice, but I recommend using Homebrew for OS X or Linux-brew for Linux specifically so you're sure to have the latest version—some package managers don't keep up with these tools' release cycles. To be clear: you're installing this software so you can use `fleetctl` and `etcdctl` from your workstation, but it's *not* intended that you'll run the fleetd and etcd daemons on your workstation.

2.2.1   *fleetctl*

As the client application for fleet, `fleetctl` gives you management over your cluster's services' states. It also manages the distribution of your systemd unit files. As mentioned earlier, you'll be using `fleetctl` on a CoreOS machine; but you can also use it remotely with SSH tunneling. Using `fleetctl` with a tunnel requires that you do some preconfiguration with SSH.

You can choose one of two options to use remote `fleetctl` with your Vagrant cluster. The best option is if you're already running `ssh-agent`:

```
host$ ssh-add ${HOME}/.vagrant.d/insecure_private_key     ⊲─┐
```
> **If you're on OS X, you may want to add -K to ssh-add, or you'll have to add it for every reboot.**

Additionally, if you're using `ssh-agent`, make sure you're forwarding your agent socket to remote hosts. In your ~/.ssh/config file, it should look something like this:

```
Host *              ⊲──────── You can lock this down to core-* if you want to.
  ForwardAgent yes
```

This ensures that your agent will be available within a CoreOS machine, once you've ssh ed to it, so it can use the same agent to talk to another CoreOS machine. If you aren't using `ssh-agent`, you can add Vagrant's SSH config to your local SSH config:

```
host$ vagrant ssh-config core-01 >> ~/.ssh/config
```

You also need to discover which port Vagrant has assigned to SSH on your host (it almost always starts with 2222):

```
host$ vagrant port core-01
The forwarded ports for the machine are listed below. Please note that
these values may differ from values configured in the Vagrantfile if the
provider supports automatic port collision detection and resolution.

    22 (guest) => 2222 (host)
```

You should now be able to ssh manually into your CoreOS node:

```
host$ ssh -p2222 core@127.0.0.1
CoreOS alpha (928.0.0)
core@core-01 ~ $
```

You should also be able to use `fleetctl` with a tunnel:

```
host$ fleetctl --tunnel=127.0.0.1:2222 list-machines
The authenticity of host '[127.0.0.1]:2222' can't be established.
RSA key fingerprint is ac:d5:6a:3f:ea:b3:47:b4:8b:74:79:09:a7:f4:33:f2.
Are you sure you want to continue connecting (yes/no)? yes     ⊲─┐
MACHINE      IP              METADATA
45b08438... 172.17.8.102    -
cac39fc1... 172.17.8.101    -             fleetctl maintains a separate, trusted
cf69ccab... 172.17.8.103    -                hosts file from your SSH config,
                                          typically in ~/.fleetctl/known_hosts.
```

You can also export an environment variable for the tunnel, if you want to type less:

```
host$ export FLEETCTL_TUNNEL=127.0.0.1:2222
```

You've already used `list-machines` in a few examples to verify that the cluster is operating normally. You'll see in the output of `list-machines` a unique hash representing a particular node in the cluster; if you want to see the full ID, you can append `--full` to `list-machines`. You can also do machine-specific operations on the short hash, such as `fleetctl ssh cac39fc1`, which will `ssh` you into that particular machine.

Let's look at how `fleetctl` interacts with unit files. We'll start with the simple example we started in chapter 1: an NGINX server. The following listing changes the example a bit to have one instance.

Listing 2.1 Single NGINX unit: code/ch2/nginx.service

```
[Unit]
Description=My Nginx Server
Requires=docker.service
After=docker.service

[Service]
ExecStartPre=-/usr/bin/docker kill mynginx
ExecStartPre=-/usr/bin/docker rm -f mynginx
ExecStartPre=/usr/bin/docker pull nginx:latest
ExecStart=/usr/bin/docker run --rm --name mynginx -p 80:80 nginx:latest
```

> These first two ExecStartPre lines ensure that you have a clean runtime. ExecStartPre lines in systemd that begin with a - after the = won't cause the unit to fail if they don't succeed. If you leave out the -, this command must exit with a 0.

> Docker runtime command

Once you've saved that, you have a few options. `fleetctl` has some commands that are effectively aliases for a few related commands.

To start a service in some way, you can use the following:

- `submit` - `fleetctl submit <unit file>` will upload the unit file to the cluster.
- `load` - `fleetctl load <unit file>` will `submit` (if needed) and assign the unit to a machine.
- `start` - `fleetctl start <unit file>` will `submit` (if needed), `load` (if needed), and start the service on the appropriate machine.

Most of the time, you'll want `start`. But `load` can be useful if you want to see *where* units will start without actually starting them; and `submit` can be handy if you just want to update your unit file and then restart the service at a later time.

> **NOTE** `fleetctl` maintains its own SSH known_hosts file in $HOME/.fleetctl/known_hosts. So, if you've ever destroyed your Vagrant cluster, new hosts may now be running on the same IPs, which may throw a known-hosts error. Clear this file.

For simplicity, you can start your service with `start`, although you're welcome to use the other two commands:

```
core@core-01 ~ $ fleetctl start code/ch2/nginx.service
Unit nginx.service inactive
Unit nginx.service launched on 45b08438.../172.17.8.102
```

Next, let's look at how to inspect some things about the current state. The first thing you can check is the status of all the units in the cluster:

```
core@core-01 ~ $ fleetctl list-units
UNIT            MACHINE                        ACTIVE   SUB
nginx.service   45b08438.../172.17.8.102       active   running
```

This shows you that NGINX has successfully started on machine 45b08438. You can inspect the status of the service as well:

fleetctl is trying to ssh into another machine. fleet knows where it's being run from and where the target service is running, and will automatically use SSH to grab that information from the other machine in the cluster.

Unit filename and description you put in line 2 of listing 2.1

```
core@core-01 ~ $ fleetctl status nginx
The authenticity of host '172.17.8.102' can't be established.
...
- nginx.service - My Nginx Server
    Loaded: loaded (/run/fleet/units/nginx.service;
      linked-runtime; vendor preset: disabled)
    Active: active (running) since Mon 2016-01-18 04:51:20 UTC;
      1min 28s ago
   Process: 1482 ExecStartPre=/usr/bin/docker pull nginx:latest
      (code=exited, status=0/SUCCESS)
   Process: 1473 ExecStartPre=/usr/bin/docker rm nginx
      (code=exited, status=1/FAILURE)
   Process: 1415 ExecStartPre=/usr/bin/docker kill nginx
      (code=exited, status=1/FAILURE)
  Main PID: 1558 (docker)
    Memory: 9.3M
       CPU: 132ms
    CGroup: /system.slice/nginx.service
            └1558 /usr/bin/docker run --name mynginx -p 80:80 nginx:latest

Jan 18 04:51:18 core-02 docker[1482]: b7a88d355049: Pull complete
...
Jan 18 04:51:20 core-02 systemd[1]: Started My Nginx Server.
```

Indicates that the unit file is loaded from this particular path, which is only important to fleet

When the service was started

PID of the Docker container

Statistical information about the main PID and its children

PID and results of each ExecStartPre line. As explained earlier, it's okay for the rm and kill ones to fail.

Beginning of the last 10 lines of the stdout of the unit file's runtime; in this case, Docker pulling NGINX from the Docker registry and starting it. This will always show the last 10 lines of output, so the output will vary. In this example, if I hit my NGINX server with curl, you'd see some HTTP logging here.

Governing CGroup, which points to a relative location you can access within sysfs (for this example, it's in /sys/fs/cgroup/systemd/system.slice/nginx.service)

> **NOTE** Although it's great that `fleetctl status` shows you a lot of information, manipulating files in /run/fleet/ and in /sys/fs/cgroup/ is well outside the scope of this book and also outside the scope of administrating CoreOS in general. If you find yourself needing to do things with these files for any reason other than your own edification and exploration, you're probably going down a road that's difficult to maintain.

Let's look at how you can use this information. First, let's get into core-02, where the service is running. `fleetctl ssh` has a handy feature that lets you `ssh` into a host by passing the service name, so you don't have to think too much about your cluster's IPs or machine IDs:

```
core@core-01 ~ $ fleetctl ssh nginx
Last login: Mon Jan 18 04:58:52 2016 from 172.17.8.101
CoreOS alpha (928.0.0)
core@core-02 ~ $
```

Now, you can `curl localhost` to see your NGINX server:

```
core@core-02 ~ $ curl -I localhost:80          ◁┄┄┄   Makes a simple request to
HTTP/1.1 200 OK                                        the running HTTP server
Server: nginx/1.9.9
...

core@core-02 ~ $ fleetctl status nginx | tail -n 5          Looks at the last
Jan 18 04:51:20 core-02 docker[1482]: 407195ab8b07: Pull complete    10 lines of
Jan 18 04:51:20 core-02 docker[1482]: Digest:         ◁              fleetctl status
    ⇒sha256:f732c04f585170ed3bc991e06404bb92504a1d25bfffa0aefd44279f35d1430c
Jan 18 04:51:20 core-02 docker[1482]: Status:
    ⇒Downloaded newer image for nginx:latest             There's the
Jan 18 04:51:20 core-02 systemd[1]: Started My Nginx Server.   curl request!
Jan 18 05:06:45 core-02 docker[1558]: 10.1.55.1 - -
    ⇒[18/Jan/2016:05:06:45 +0000] "HEAD / HTTP/1.1" 200 0 "-" "curl/7.43.0" "-"
```

> **NOTE** If the `fleetctl status nginx` command fails with something about `SSH_AUTH_SOCK`, you probably didn't add `ForwardAgent yes` to your SSH config.

Another great informational feature is access to the journal. As you may know, systemd uses journaled logging, which has the benefit of not filling up your filesystem with logs. I'm sure, as a professional, you've never had a server go down from having a filesystem full of logs (haha!). fleet has full access to this journal from any node, as well as the ability to `follow` the log as you would have done in the past with `tail -f`:

```
core@core-01 ~ $ fleetctl journal -f nginx
-- Logs begin at Sun 2016-01-17 20:48:02 UTC. --
Jan 18 04:51:20 core-02 docker[1482]: 38267e0e16c7: Pull complete
Jan 18 04:51:20 core-02 docker[1482]: 407195ab8b07: Pull complete
... etc
```

Now, you can remove your service. Much like starting it, there's the same set of encompassing commands: stop, unload, and destroy. destroy both stops and unloads as well as completely removes the service files, and unload both stops and unloads the service. Let's look at these in sequence to better understand the states.

Here, the NGINX service is loaded but not running:

```
core@core-01 ~ $ fleetctl stop nginx
Unit nginx.service loaded on 45b08438.../172.17.8.102
core@core-01 ~ $ fleetctl list-units
UNIT            MACHINE                        ACTIVE  SUB
nginx.service   45b08438.../172.17.8.102       failed  failed
```

Next, the NGINX service is removed from fleet's registry, but the unit file is still available:

```
core@core-01 ~ $ fleetctl unload nginx
Unit nginx.service inactive
core@core-01 ~ $ fleetctl list-units
UNIT    MACHINE ACTIVE  SUB
core@core-01 ~ $ fleetctl list-unit-files
UNIT            HASH     DSTATE        STATE        TARGET
nginx.service   fbf621b  inactive      inactive     -
```

And finally, the NGINX service is completely destroyed:

```
core@core-01 ~ $ fleetctl destroy nginx
Destroyed nginx.service
core@core-01 ~ $ fleetctl list-unit-files
UNIT    HASH    DSTATE  STATE   TARGET
core@core-01 ~ $
```

You should now be pretty comfortable with how fleetctl functions and have an understanding of how to access information you need to use and administer services in CoreOS. To recap, you've done the following:

- Created a simple systemd unit file for NGINX
- Deployed the unit file to your CoreOS cluster
- Learned how to extract information from your service
- Removed the NGINX service from your cluster

Next, we can move on to the other crucial bit of cluster state: etcd!

2.2.2   *etcdctl*

etcdctl is the user-space tool for manipulating etcd. As the name implies, it's a daemon to store cluster-wide configuration. Everything you can do with etcdctl, you can also do with curl; it just provides a friendly wrapper around accessing and changing information.

The etcd cluster is available to any machine in the CoreOS cluster. You *can* make it available within a running container, but you should understand the security implications of doing so. The latest version of etcd has basic role-based access control (RBAC) to grant and restrict certain subcommands; we'll get deeper into configuring etcd later in the book. For now, we'll look at the basics of using etcdctl for service registration and discovery, which are the most common usage scenarios.

You can begin by exploring your etcd directory recursively:

```
core@core-01 ~ $ etcdctl ls --recursive /
/coreos.com
/coreos.com/updateengine
/coreos.com/updateengine/rebootlock
/coreos.com/updateengine/rebootlock/semaphore
/coreos.com/network
/coreos.com/network/config
/coreos.com/network/subnets
/coreos.com/network/subnets/10.1.42.0-24
/coreos.com/network/subnets/10.1.55.0-24
/coreos.com/network/subnets/10.1.16.0-24
```

The top-level coreos.com/ key is populated and managed by etcd and CoreOS.

The coreos.com/updateengine key contains a semaphore for the rolling CoreOS upgrade process (we'll go into the upgrade process in chapter 3).

The coreos.com/network key contains basic network information.

You can get any of these endpoints, and they will return some JSON:

```
core@core-01 ~ $ etcdctl get /coreos.com/network/config
{ "Network": "10.1.0.0/16" }
core@core-01 ~ $ etcdctl get /coreos.com/network/subnets/10.1.42.0-24
{ "PublicIP": "172.17.8.103" }
```

This path will probably be different for you, so look at the output of the previous example's command if you want to try it.

You may already see how some of this information can be useful for things like load balancers and networking configuration outside of the cluster.

Just as easily as getting information with etcdctl, you can set information, as well:

```
core@core-01 ~ $ etcdctl set /foo/bar '{ "baz": "quux" }'
{ "baz": "quux" }
```

You can also set a time-to-live (TTL) for any value:

```
core@core-01 ~ $ etcdctl set --ttl 3 /foo/bar '{ "baz": "quux" }'; \
> sleep 1; \
> etcdctl get /foo/bar; \
> sleep 3; \
> etcdctl get /foo/bar
{ "baz": "quux" }
{ "baz": "quux" }
Error:  100: Key not found (/foo/bar) [24861]
```

You'll remember from chapter 1 that the sidekick examples used a TTL of 60 seconds so that you could retain the value slightly longer than the loop sleep time to set it again. Tuning this value is important for configuring when things like load-balancer health checks run, or how long you want some kinds of failure to remain in a particular state.

etcdctl watch and watch-exec can also be used in creative ways to monitor and set configurations for live services. We'll go into more detail on how to use these features later in the book. We'll also go deeper into configuring etcd later; for now, knowing these basic commands is enough to get started. As you can see, etcd has a simple interface to a distributed configuration with a lot of potential. By default, any query run against the cluster will ensure that the data is in sync before it returns, so it guarantees consistency and accuracy above all else.

etcdctl and fleetctl are the tools specific to CoreOS that you'll use all the time. But as I'm sure you know, a whole world of Linux tools and commands are available to do various things in an operating system. This is where the Toolbox comes into play.

2.2.3   *The Toolbox container*

CoreOS has a strict philosophy of being a very static system. There's no package manager installed, and you should never rely on the local filesystem to maintain anything; etcd and fleet are the only places you store any kind of state. But sometimes you need to debug something from within the cluster—say, you need to run nmap to try to figure out why you can't reach another host on your network from CoreOS.

This is where the Toolbox comes in. Essentially, the Toolbox is a basic Fedora Linux Docker container where you can install and use all the tools you're used to for administration. You install and use the Toolbox as follows:

```
core@core-01 ~ $ toolbox              ◁─────┐ Downloads the Toolbox Docker container
...                                          │ and executes it in your terminal
latest: Pulling from library/fedora
Spawning container core-fedora-latest on /var/lib/toolbox/core-fedora-latest.
Press ^] three times within 1s to kill container.
[root@core-01 ~]# dnf install nmap    ◁─────┐ You're now in a Fedora Linux container
...                                          │ and can use dnf to install nmap.
Complete!
root@core-01 ~]# nmap -p80 google.com                              ◁─────────────┐
                                                                                 │
Starting Nmap 7.00 ( https://nmap.org ) at 2016-01-18 06:54 UTC                  │
...
80/tcp open  http

Normal-looking dnf installation                            Now you can use nmap as
output omitted                                                 you normally would.
```

Further, your entire filesystem is mounted within the Toolbox container. So, if you want to install and use Emacs to edit files in the core home directory, you can find it mounted in /media/root:

```
core@core-01 ~ $ toolbox
Spawning container core-fedora-latest on /var/lib/toolbox/core-fedora-latest.
Press ^] three times within 1s to kill container.
[root@core-01 ~]# touch /media/root/home/core/fromtoolbox
[root@core-01 ~]# logout
Container core-fedora-latest exited successfully.
core@core-01 ~ $ ls
fromtoolbox
```

Remember, though, that although your Toolbox will persist for the life of the machine, an update will clobber anything you save there. It's meant only for debugging. Resist the temptation to use the Toolbox to serve anything or perform tasks that require its persistence.

> **A note about the Toolbox**
>
> Don't forget that the Toolbox image will take up about 200 MB of disk, which is a lot considering how small CoreOS is to begin with. You can always use `docker rmi fedora` to clean it up completely.
>
> Remember, though, that the goal with CoreOS is that you only ever need to `ssh` into a machine for development or for serious debugging needs. If you find yourself using the Toolbox frequently or for some repeated tasks, you may want to consider how you can automate your task with etcd and fleet.

2.2.4 *Conceptual shift for Linux admins*

Some conceptual changes Linux admins face are probably obvious, given the circumstances in which you'd use the Toolbox (for example, just as a utility, not a workstation environment). There's no package manager in CoreOS by design, and poking around in the OS from a terminal session on the host isn't something you should do or have to do on a regular basis. You should consider all the data on any particular filesystem of any given machine to be ephemeral and unimportant on its own. If you're already used to working with public cloud systems, this shouldn't be too much of a hurdle.

THINKING ABOUT DATA PERSISTENCE

Dealing with that ephemeral state can be a little daunting, and I'm sure your first thought is, "Then how do I do databases?" The answer is a bit complex and depends on the technologies you're using. Some data systems handle this architecture within their own design (Elasticsearch, Riak, Mongo, and so on), and others will probably need some help (such as PostgreSQL). As a general rule, software that's designed to scale horizontally will be easier to implement here than software that isn't. For the latter, there are a few solutions that we'll get into later in the book.

TRADITIONAL USER MANAGEMENT AND OS CONFIGURATION

Because you almost never `ssh` into a machine to do anything for administration, you'll also find that you won't need to be too concerned with managing users and permissions in CoreOS. If you find you really, really, need to do that kind of thing, it's possible, but expect your cloud-config to become more complex.

You'll also notice the lack of configuration management in general. I touched on this in chapter 1, but the initial state is always defined by cloud-config. Beyond this initial state, there isn't much to do unless you're debugging or testing things in your local test cluster, and therefore there's no need for traditional configuration-management suites (Puppet, Chef, and so on). It's entirely possible for you to set up cloud-config to bootstrap Chef, but the point of CoreOS isn't to alter the state of a machine once it's up, and doing so would serve little purpose.

UPDATES AND GENERAL SYSTEM ADMINISTRATION

Another aspect of normal system administration that you may be wondering about is updates. Configuration management or something you have to set up has probably been your go-to for keeping systems up at scale; what's happening for CoreOS?

If you've spun up your development cluster following the instructions in this chapter, and it's been running a few days on your workstation, and if you're a very observant person, you may have noticed the login message change when you sshed into a machine: for example, from CoreOS alpha (928.0.0) to CoreOS alpha (933.0.0). Or, you may see that your machine's uptime doesn't match how long you know you've been running this cluster. CoreOS updates itself. It does so by installing the new version on a "B" partition and rebooting one machine at a time in the cluster. This method solves a number of problems with update management, and it's also a tunable process that we'll go into in much more depth later.

2.3   Summary

- CoreOS officially supports and maintains the tools to run your development environment, available via GitHub.
- A CoreOS virtualized development environment provides a sandbox in which you can simulate anything you would do in a production CoreOS deployment.
- You can use this environment to test and debug new systemd unit files so you find issues early.
- Using etcd, you can develop consistent integrations between your services as well as to any external system.
- With your development cluster, you can model how fleet will distribute your application stack.
- OS updates and normal Linux system administration tasks are minimized or nonexistent in CoreOS.

Expecting failure: fault tolerance in CoreOS

This chapter covers

- Monitoring and fault tolerance in CoreOS
- Getting your first complex service running
- Application architecture in the context of CoreOS

If you work in infrastructure or operations in any capacity, you'll understand the importance of monitoring systems. When the alarms go off, it's time to figure out what's happened. You might have also taken a crack at automating some of the most common fixes to problems or mitigated situations with disaster-recovery failover switches, multicasting, or a variety of other ways to react to failure. You probably also have an understanding that technology always finds a way to break. Hardware, software, connectivity, power grid—these are all things that wake us up in the middle of the night. If you've been working in operations for a while, you probably have the sense that although automating fault tolerance is possible, it's usually risky and difficult to maintain.

CoreOS tries to solve this problem; by providing generic abstractions for the state of your application distributed over a cluster, the implementation details of automating fault tolerance become much clearer and reusable. The next logical benefit of containers after abstracting the runtime from any particular machine is to allow that runtime to be portable across a network, thus decoupling any container from the failure of its host.

In this chapter, we'll expand on what you learned in chapters 1 and 2 and dive into more-complex examples of how to give your services greater resiliency and quicker failure recovery. We'll examine how to manage the ephemeral nature of application stacks and explore some high-level concepts of systems architecture and design and how they apply to CoreOS. By the end of this chapter, you'll have a good understanding of how to plan deployments of your applications to CoreOS; this will lead into chapter 4, where we'll move to production.

3.1 The current state of monitoring

If you've been in operations for any length of time, you've used some kind of monitoring system. Usually such systems look like the typical monitoring architectures shown in figures 3.1 and 3.2, or a combination.

Your monitoring system can either send out probes to gather information about a server and its services, as in figure 3.1, and/or an agent running on the server can report status to a monitoring system, as in figure 3.2. You've probably experienced the drawbacks of each approach. Probes are difficult to maintain, and they fire false positives; and agents can be just as difficult to maintain, while also adding load to your system and uncertainty around the agent's reliability. With etcd, CoreOS replaces much of the need for these systems by normalizing state information that's composed by the services.

With traditional monitoring setups, you usually assume that your monitoring system is at least as reliable as the thing it's monitoring. Sometimes you rely on third-party solutions for monitoring, and other times you end up monitoring your own monitoring system. As your infrastructure and applications grow, your monitoring

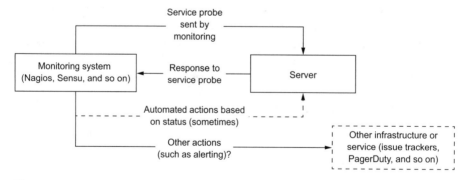

Figure 3.1 Monitoring with probes

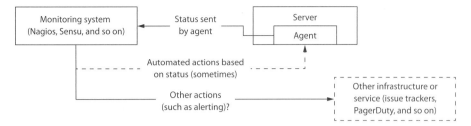

Figure 3.2   Monitoring with an agent

solutions increase in complexity right along with them; at the end of the day, monitoring tells you about the state of everything at once and usually doesn't do a great job of telling you why the state changed. If you're using things like public clouds, sometimes you can't even find out or don't care why it changed.

CoreOS lets you take a different approach to retaining observation of your live systems. To be clear, CoreOS doesn't do anything to preclude monitoring. What it *does* do is free your time to allow you to focus on monitoring what's important (your application), and not what isn't. (You're not in the business of maintaining operating systems, right?)

3.1.1   *What's lacking*

Consider this scenario. Your company runs a business-critical Rails application, and a cluster of Debian servers keeps it running. Maybe you've even got Chef keeping all the configurations in line. You've spent hours ensuring that log files are shipped off to a third-party log consumer.

One night, you get an alert from your monitoring system that that disks are full and your application isn't responding. Root-cause analysis time! Did the update you ran last month overwrite some of your log configs and begin writing logs to disk again? Did that new developer decide to write a new log file and not let you know? Did you miss something in your Chef config a year ago that slowly leaked data to disk where it shouldn't be? Is it a false positive? (Don't lie: you know the first thing you'd do is run df to see if the monitoring system was playing a trick on you.)

Finally, you find out you weren't purging your .deb files out of /var/cache often enough after you added a little automation around OS upgrades. A very small log file was being written to every day from a short cron job you added six months ago, and the combination brought everything down. At this point, you ask yourself, "What does any of this have to do with the application I'm supporting?" and "Why am I still solving the same system administration problems I was solving 10 years ago?"

Monitoring has become the tip of the iceberg—or maybe a better metaphor is a canary in a coal mine, reminding you that you missed an edge case. Can you keep up with edge cases as fast as they're created?

3.1.2   *What CoreOS does differently*

CoreOS takes back the responsibility of not letting your OS or its configuration be the downfall of your application:

- It's stripped down to eliminate a lot of configuration and administration problems out of the box.
- As we discussed in chapter 1, CoreOS takes advantage of containerization's ability to abstract your application from the OS, as well as as abstract it from the machine with fleet, to empower you to focus on your application and not OS internals.
- Application failures are contained, and machine failures are mitigated so that they can be handled outside of a maintenance window (or ignored in some public cloud scenarios).
- Maintenance of the OS is also done without the need for interaction.

You can forget the fear of OS upgrades for two reasons. First, the behavior of a CoreOS operating system upgrade from the perspective of your application is the same as the behavior of a machine outage: that downtime is avoided by fleet shifting around containers across the cluster to meet your specifications, regardless of the state of the cluster. And second, *because* everything is abstracted by containers, nothing in your application depends on anything in the base OS being available other than the handful of CoreOS services.

With these benefits in mind, see how figure 3.3 shows a CoreOS upgrade in progress. Although this level of OS automation might seem dangerous, the abstraction afforded by containers and fleet significantly reduces the impact. Essentially, this is CoreOS dogfooding its approach to providing fault tolerance for your applications onto the OS. The upgrade process is part of the equation of how CoreOS reduces the need for complex monitoring systems; the cluster-wide scheduling and discovery systems reveal a much more generic interface for gathering important data.

The default setting for upgrade-locking (`etcd-lock`) is to have only one machine upgrade in the cluster at a time. If the etcd cluster is in a problematic state, it won't upgrade any nodes. If you have a larger cluster, you can increase the number of nodes that can upgrade and reboot simultaneously with `locksmithctl`:

```
core@core-01 $ locksmithctl set-max 2
Old: 1
New: 2
```

> **NOTE** Don't actually do this on your local three-node cluster! If two out of three nodes reboot at the same time, you'll lose the quorum in etcd. A quorum in etcd can tolerate up to $(N\text{-}1)/2$ failures, where N is the number of cluster members (machines).

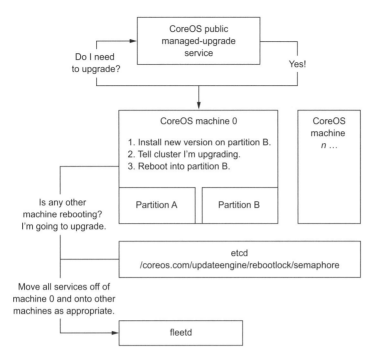

Figure 3.3 CoreOS upgrade process

Cluster upgrades

CoreOS operating system upgrades require some level of public internet access to *.release.core-os.net by default, via either an HTTP proxy or NAT. If you want more control over upgrades beyond the three release channels, CoreOS, Inc. (the company) provides a premium managed service to assist you.

Additionally, how you plan the capacity of your services should go hand in hand with how you plan your cluster and upgrade configuration. Upgrades will occur only when etcd has an available lock and has no errors (for example, another machine is down or rebooting for some reason other than an upgrade). If your services can't all live on a cluster with the performance you expect while missing two nodes, don't increase your `etcd-lock` max. But at a *minimum* you should plan for one machine outage. This isn't much different from scaling mass storage: the more redundant units, the higher your fault tolerance to some kinds of failure.

3.2 Service scheduling and discovery

In chapters 1 and 2, you learned a bit about etcd and fleet and how they provide service scheduling and discovery for your application. Together, they provide fault tolerance and composability for monitoring data within your application runtime, rather than from outside of it. We'll go a little deeper here and consider a more realistic example to illustrate how these things can fit together. We'll expand on the NGINX example with an upstream Express example application, and we'll look at how to further use etcd in this application stack. In this example, NGINX will monitor the state of the Express application and act accordingly without the need for an outside monitoring system.

To observe how CoreOS can hedge your services against failure, you'll build out an application environment with fault tolerance built in. Then, you'll try to break it with partial failures in the cluster and observe how the fault tolerance reacts.

3.2.1 Deploying production NGINX and Express

A real-world example would involve at least a couple of tiers. We won't get into the complexities of database tiers yet (we will later!), but an application stack isn't really a stack unless some internal communication is going on. Say, for example, that you want to deploy an application that consists of some Express node services behind an instance of NGINX. Ultimately, you want your system to look like figure 3.4, which shows the simple network topology between NGINX and the Express applications behind it.

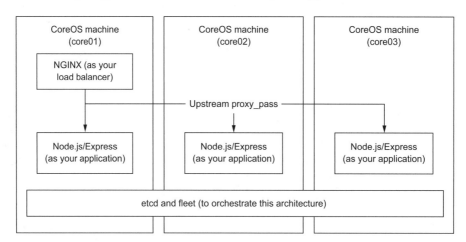

Figure 3.4   NGINX and Express stack

In this scenario, NGINX acts like a load balancer but could be performing any number of jobs (SSL termination, external reverse proxies, and so on). The next few sections set up this architecture; it's crucial for you to take away that the failure of any node becomes a non-concern as you build toward a fault-tolerant application instead of a monitoring-dependent one.

3.2.2 Using etcd for configuration

For this application stack, you'll use what you learned in chapter 2: you'll set up NGINX in a CoreOS cluster and add a fairly common back-end service. The example uses Node.js/Express mostly for simplicity, but it could be any HTTP service you want to distribute across your cluster.

I've added some significant complexity to the previous example, in the form of a new requirement to modify and deploy containers that are different from the publicly available Docker images. But I'll assume that you have a repository to which to upload custom built containers and that you're using the public, official Docker registry at https://hub.docker.com.

For the sake of the example, assume that it's okay to publish your containers to Docker's public repository. In the real world, of course, this might not be possible. There are many options for publishing private Docker images, using software-as-a-service (SaaS) products or hosting your own repository, but that's beyond the scope of this book. For further reading, check out *Docker in Action* by Jeff Nickoloff (Manning, 2016, www.manning.com/books/docker-in-action).

THE EXPRESS APPLICATION

Let's start with your Express instance. First you need to create a "Hello World" Express app. You don't need any experience with Node.js for this; you can paste the code from listings 3.1, 3.2, and 3.3 into files in a new directory.

Listing 3.1   code/ch3/helloworld/app.js

```
const app = require('express')()
app.get('/', (req, res) => { res.send('hello world').end() })
app.listen(3000)
```

Listing 3.2   code/ch3/helloworld/Dockerfile

```
FROM node:5-onbuild
EXPOSE 3000
```

Listing 3.3   code/ch3/helloworld/package.json

```
{
  "name": "helloworld",
  "scripts": {
    "start": "node app.js"
  },
  "dependencies": {
    "express": "^4"
  }
}
```

Next, build the image and push it to the Docker hub. You can do all this on a CoreOS instance (because it has Docker running) or anywhere else you may be running Docker, such as your workstation:

```
$ cd code/ch3/helloworld
$ docker build -t mattbailey/helloworld .
Sending build context to Docker daemon 1.166 MB
...
Successfully built f8945e023a8c

$ docker login  # IF NECESSARY
$ docker push mattbailey/helloworld
```

```
The push refers to a repository [docker.io/mattbailey/helloworld]
...
latest: digest: sha256:e803[...]190e size: 12374
```

You can drop your .service files in this directory as well. It's somewhat common to keep these service files under the same source control as the project. You'll have a main service file and a sidekick.

The first service file looks at lot like what you saw with NGINX, but you reference the Docker image you published earlier.

Listing 3.4   code/ch3/helloworld/helloworld@.service

```
[Unit]
Description=Hello World Service
Requires=docker.service
After=docker.service

[Service]
TimeoutStartSec=0
ExecStartPre=-/usr/bin/docker kill helloworld
ExecStartPre=-/usr/bin/docker rm -f helloworld
ExecStartPre=/usr/bin/docker pull mattbailey/helloworld:latest
ExecStart=/usr/bin/docker run --name helloworld \
  -p 3000:3000 mattbailey/helloworld:latest
ExecStop=-/usr/bin/docker stop helloworld

[X-Fleet]
Conflicts=helloworld@*
```

> ### What is TimeoutStartSec?
>
> Notice that you use `TimeoutStartSec=0` in listing 3.4, to indicate that you don't want a timeout for this service. This can be helpful on slower connections or with larger Docker images that may take a while to pull, especially if you're pulling them all at the same time in three VMs on a single workstation.
>
> You may want to tune this setting in the future depending on your use cases (you could, for example, set it from etcd), but it's easier to have no timeout while you're testing and developing services.

The sidekick also looks similar: it announces the presence of the `helloworld` service in /services/helloworld/.

Listing 3.5   code/ch3/helloworld/helloworld-sidekick@.service

```
[Unit]
Description=Register Hello World %i
BindsTo=helloworld@%i.service
After=helloworld@%i.service

[Service]
TimeoutStartSec=0
```

```
EnvironmentFile=/etc/environment
ExecStartPre=/usr/bin/etcdctl set /services/changed/helloworld 1
ExecStart=/bin/bash -c 'while true; \
  do \
    [ "`etcdctl get /services/helloworld/${COREOS_PUBLIC_IPV4}`" \
      != "server ${COREOS_PUBLIC_IPV4}:3000;" ] && \
    etcdctl set /services/changed/helloworld 1; \
    etcdctl set /services/helloworld/${COREOS_PUBLIC_IPV4} \
      \'server ${COREOS_PUBLIC_IPV4}:3000;\' \
      --ttl 60;sleep 45;done'
ExecStop=/usr/bin/etcdctl rm /services/helloworld/helloworld@%i
ExecStopPost=/usr/bin/etcdctl set /services/changed/helloworld 1

[X-Fleet]
MachineOf=helloworld@%i.service
```

Organizing etcd keys

There are no strict guidelines or preset structures for how to organize your etcd keys—doing so is completely free-form.

You will, of course, want to plan this structure much as you'd plan your infrastructure, to keep things appropriately namespaced and flexible enough to accommodate your future needs.

Now, you can fire up `helloworld` on your cluster and verify that it has started:

```
$ fleetctl start code/ch3/helloworld/helloworld@{1..3}.service
Unit helloworld@1.service inactive
Unit helloworld@2.service inactive
Unit helloworld@3.service inactive
$ fleetctl start code/ch3/helloworld/helloworld-sidekick@{1..3}.service
Unit helloworld-sidekick@1.service inactive
Unit helloworld-sidekick@2.service inactive
Unit helloworld-sidekick@3.service inactive
```

Also, verify that `helloworld` is running:

```
$ fleetctl list-units
UNIT              MACHINE        ACTIVE  SUB
helloworld-sidekick@1.service a12d26db.../172.17.8.102  active  running
helloworld-sidekick@2.service c1fc6b79.../172.17.8.103  active  running
helloworld-sidekick@3.service c37d052c.../172.17.8.101  active  running
helloworld@1.service    a12d26db.../172.17.8.102  active  running
helloworld@2.service    c1fc6b79.../172.17.8.103  active  running
helloworld@3.service    c37d052c.../172.17.8.101  active  running
$ curl 172.17.8.101:3000
hello world
$ etcdctl ls /services/helloworld/
/services/helloworld/172.17.8.101
/services/helloworld/172.17.8.103
/services/helloworld/172.17.8.102
```

The next section moves on to the NGINX configuration.

THE NGINX APPLICATION

Create a new directory for your NGINX build. You'll have three files for configuring NGINX, not including the service units. The first is a fairly simple Dockerfile using the official NGINX image as its base.

Listing 3.6 code/ch3/nginx/Dockerfile

```
FROM nginx

COPY helloworld.conf /tmp/helloworld.conf
COPY start.sh /tmp/start.sh
RUN chmod +x /tmp/start.sh

EXPOSE 80

CMD ["/tmp/start.sh"]
```

Next is a start script. You'll using Bash as the dynamic runtime configuration for simplicity, so you won't add any more dependencies to the example. But many tools are available to help you template your configuration files at runtime, such as confd (www.confd.io).

Listing 3.7 code/ch3/nginx/start.sh

```
#!/usr/bin/env bash

# Write dynamic nginx config
echo "upstream helloworld { ${UPSTREAM} }" > /etc/nginx/conf.d/default.conf

# Write rest of static config
cat /tmp/helloworld.conf >> /etc/nginx/conf.d/default.conf

# Now start nginx
nginx -g 'daemon off;'
```

Finally, here's the static NGINX config file for the reverse proxy.

Listing 3.8 code/ch3/nginx/helloworld.conf

```
server {
    listen      80;
    location / {
        proxy_pass http://helloworld;
    }
}
```

Build and push this image to your repository, just as you did the Express app:

```
$ cd code/ch3/nginx/
$ docker build -t mattbailey/helloworld-nginx .
Sending build context to Docker daemon 4.096 kB
...
Successfully built e9cfe4f5f144

$ docker push mattbailey/helloworld-nginx
```

```
The push refers to a repository [docker.io/mattbailey/helloworld-nginx]
...
latest: digest: sha256:01e4[...]81f8 size: 7848
```

Now, you can write your service files, shown in listings 3.9 and 3.10.

Listing 3.9   code/ch3/nginx/helloworld-nginx.service

```
[Unit]
Description=Hello World Nginx
Requires=docker.service
After=docker.service

[Service]
TimeoutStartSec=0
ExecStartPre=-/usr/bin/docker kill helloworld-nginx
ExecStartPre=-/usr/bin/docker rm -f helloworld-nginx
ExecStartPre=/usr/bin/docker pull mattbailey/helloworld-nginx:latest
ExecStart=/bin/sh -c /for host in `etcdctl ls /services/helloworld`; \
  do UPSTREAM=$UPSTREAM`etcdctl get $host`; \
  done; \
  docker run -t -e UPSTREAM="$UPSTREAM" \
    --name helloworld-nginx -p 80:80 mattbailey/helloworld-nginx:latest'
ExecStop=-/usr/bin/docker stop helloworld-nginx
```

Listing 3.10   code/ch3/nginx/helloworld-nginx-sidekick.service

```
[Unit]
Description=Restart Nginx On Change

[Service]
ExecStart=/usr/bin/etcdctl exec-watch \
  /services/changed/helloworld -- \
  /bin/sh -c "fleetctl stop helloworld-nginx.service; \
  fleetctl start helloworld-nginx.service"
```

Next, start your NGINX service units:

```
$ fleetctl start code/ch3/nginx/helloworld-nginx.service
Unit helloworld-nginx.service inactive
Unit helloworld-nginx.service launched on a12d26db.../172.17.8.102
$ fleetctl start code/ch3/nginx/helloworld-nginx-sidekick.service
Unit helloworld-nginx-sidekick.service inactive
Unit helloworld-nginx-sidekick.service launched on a12d26db.../172.17.8.102
```

Notice that you don't care which machine the sidekick runs on for NGINX, because it's interacting with NGINX entirely via `etcdctl` and `fleetctl`.

You should now have a setup that looks like figure 3.4. NGINX is effectively watching for changes in the topology of Express applications and is set up to adapt to those changes. Further, you did this without implementing any complex monitoring systems. You expect failure to occur, and CoreOS lets you integrate that notion into the composition of the service architecture. You need to test this notion; so, in the next section, you'll see what happens when a machine fails.

3.3   Breaking things

Now that you have a "production-like" deployment in place, it's time to try to break it! What you've built should stand up pretty well to a single machine failure. We'll look at how a machine failure affects your application and the how CoreOS can bring the cluster back together when it's restored. Simulating more complex scenarios is a little difficult on a local cluster of three machines; but as a baseline, the CoreOS cluster considers any inability to resolve a node in etcd as a machine failure and will react as if a machine is down. As mentioned in section 3.1.2, etcd can survive $(N\text{-}1)/2$ machine failures, where N is the number of machines; because etcd is the source of truth for your cluster state, your deployment of CoreOS machines (virtual or physical) should consider this rate of failure a baseline.

3.3.1   Simulating a machine failure

The most destructive kind of scenario you can simulate is a complete failure of a CoreOS machine. This scenario includes loss of network connectivity, because that's functionally equivalent to the CoreOS cluster. To simulate this, you'll have to shut down one of your machines. To make things interesting, you'll shut down the machine that's also running NGINX, which will result in an outage, but one that is mitigated by fleet. You may want to open another terminal to a machine you're not shutting down to watch what happens:

```
$ vagrant ssh core-01
core@core-01 ~ $ fleetctl journal -f helloworld-nginx.service
...
Feb 17 05:00:59 core-02 systemd[1]: Started Hello World Nginx.
```

> **When failure isn't "failure"**
>
> In some scenarios, losing a machine in your cluster is intentional and doesn't represent a fault of any kind. For example, this happens if you have CoreOS automatic OS updates enabled, or you need to shut down some infrastructure for maintenance, or you want to rebuild your AWS EC2 instance for any number of reasons. If you consider machine "faults" to be occurrences that are part of the normal lifecycle of your systems, you'll have a much easier time gaining the benefits of CoreOS.

In a different terminal from your host, have Vagrant shut down the machine where `helloworld-nginx.service` is running:

```
$ vagrant halt core-02
```

Watch on core-01 or any other machine that wasn't running `helloworld-nginx.service`:

```
...
Connection to 127.0.0.1 closed by remote host.
Error running remote command: wait: remote command exited without exit status
    or exit signal
```

```
core@core-01 ~ $ fleetctl journal -f helloworld-nginx.service
...
Feb 17 05:16:32 core-01 systemd[1]: Started Hello World Nginx.
```

You can see that the service was shut down on core-02, and then fleet moved it to core-01. You can also observe that NGINX has picked up the new upstream configuration:

```
core@core-01 ~ $ docker exec -it helloworld-
    nginx cat /etc/nginx/conf.d/default.conf
upstream helloworld { server 172.17.8.101:3000;server 172.17.8.103:3000; }
server {
    listen       80;
    location / {
        proxy_pass http://helloworld;
    }
}
```

Now that you've seen your application stack adapt to a missing machine, in the next section you'll bring the machine back to see how the cluster deals with service restoration.

3.3.2 *Self-repair*

Bring the machine back up, and watch everything go back to normal:

```
$ vagrant up core-02
```

Once it's booted back up, wait about 45 seconds. Then you can confirm that the machine is back in NGINX's upstream:

```
core@core-01 ~ $ docker exec -it helloworld-
    nginx cat /etc/nginx/conf.d/default.conf
upstream helloworld { server 172.17.8.101:3000;server 172.17.8.103:3000;
    server 172.17.8.102:3000; }
server {
    listen       80;
    location / {
        proxy_pass http://helloworld;
    }
}
```

The upstream is again pointing to all three of your Express applications. It took relatively little engineering to add fault tolerance to a system completely unfamiliar with that concept. Additionally, you didn't need to employ any additional tools to accomplish this, other than what is provided by CoreOS. Ultimately, building robust, self-repairing systems is always a hard problem, but CoreOS provides a generic tool set with fleet and etcd that gives you a pattern for building it into many scenarios.

Application architecture is still an important skill. And adapting your architecture to CoreOS requires some planning, as we'll discuss next.

3.4   Application architectures and CoreOS

Application architecture is a topic that could fill many volumes. This won't be the last time we discuss it in this book; but it's worth looking at it and at how it relates to the big picture, now that you've simulated things that application architects try to plan for.

First we'll look at some common pitfalls with designing applications for failure, and then we'll follow up with a discussion of what parts of the architecture you can control. Finally, we'll touch on what all this means with respect to configuration management.

3.4.1   Common pitfalls

There are some common pitfalls when it comes to running application stacks in environments where faults are common or expected, or where the scale of what you're doing statistically demands that faults will occur at some regular interval. You can probably recognize in the chapter's example that the host on which NGINX is running becomes somewhat of a single point of failure. Even though you've designed the system to tolerate that machine's failure by starting up NGINX on another instance, you still could have a gap in availability. You can resolve this in your architecture in a few ways:

- The NGINX sidekick can update a DNS entry with a short TTL if you can tolerate a minute of downtime.
- You can rely on upstream content delivery network (CDN) caching to carry you through an outage.
- You can run NGINX on two or all three machines and have a load-balancer appliance or something like AWS Elastic Load Balancer (ELB) with a health check in front of them.

Most commonly, the last option is used if you need that level of reliability. You're building enough vertical capacity into your machines to run both services at the same time, so there's little reason not to. But here's where you have to be careful. Assume that NGINX is doing something specific for a user's session. This isn't likely; but for the sake of an example, if NGINX stored some kind of state locally, that state wouldn't be shared to the other NGINX service running on the other machine. Often, you accept that users may be logged out if some part of a cluster fails, but you also wouldn't want them to be logged out by hitting a different node behind your load balancer.

The architectural choices you make, especially with respect to the software you use, have an effect on your ability to make the architecture fault tolerant with CoreOS's tools. Even the complexity of applying fault tolerance to software that supports it can be difficult. For example, before Redis 3.0 and the `redis-cluster` feature that comes with it, clustering Redis involved a separate sentinel process to elect a write master and realign the cluster. The Redis Sentinel system was designed to be applied in a fault-tolerant system like CoreOS, but making it work was a complex task. The takeaway is that you should *always* test your cluster configurations and fault scenarios in an environment like a local Vagrant cluster, where you can control conditions.

3.4.2 *Greenfield and legacy systems*

Sometimes you get to choose your architecture, and sometimes you don't. Dealing with legacy systems is part of every engineer's career; obviously, it will be easier to build fault tolerance into a greenfield project via CoreOS than to build it into a legacy stack. You may find that it's impossible to reach certain levels of reliability in some systems that you could with others. You can, however, mitigate some of the risk with the patterns CoreOS provides.

Mostly you'll run into issues with legacy services that store some kind of state and have no way to distribute it. Of those, the single most annoying problem is the "undistributable" state being stored on the local filesystem. If the data that's being stored isn't important, the only downside is that you can only run the service on one machine; you can still rely on fleet to move it around. If the data *is* important, and you can't change how it works, you'll have to implement distributed storage. We'll go into detail about your options in section 4.5.

3.4.3 *Configuration management*

If you're dealing with greenfield applications, your approach to configuration management should assume that the application configuration is split between configuration that needs to understand the runtime environment (such as database IPs) and configuration that's stateless (such as a database driver). The former should be managed with etcd, and the latter should be managed with your container build process. With that in mind, you'll no longer need complex configuration-management systems, and your software environment will become much more repeatable and understandable.

3.5 *Summary*

- Follow the sidekick pattern to build complex application environments with service discovery.
- Use service discovery to implement fault tolerance and self-healing capabilities.
- Design scenarios in which you can simulate failures that you might see in a production environment, so you can test your cluster implementations.
- Application architectures are important in planning your CoreOS deployments and always require review.

Part 2

Application architecture

Chapters 4–7 dive deep into application architecture concepts and how they apply to CoreOS's computing model. You'll build increasingly complex software stacks on your local cluster, using the example in chapter 3 as a foundation. Your application will go from a simple "Hello World" to a multilayer, real-time application with a scalable, fault-tolerant persistent database.

CoreOS in production

This chapter covers

- CoreOS deployment options
- Networking layers to support your systems
- Large-scale persistent storage

In chapter 3, we talked about how to achieve some fault tolerance using CoreOS's features; bringing everything together into production is, of course, more complex. You have an unsurprisingly wide range of options to choose from in terms of how and where you want to deploy CoreOS and how you and your organization will maintain it long term. This chapter covers the planning and information gathering you'll need to do in a few of the most common scenarios.

The first section of the chapter goes through the things you should consider when you're planning deployments on IaaS services, in-house VMs, and bare metal. Then we'll move on to how to approach the network topology and how to think about mass storage and large data sets within your cluster.

> **NOTE** To be prepared for this chapter, you should have a basic understanding of networking and storage and at least some notion of your target for deployment.

4.1   *Planning and deployment options*

CoreOS supports a wide range of deployment options, both those supported by the CoreOS organization and community-supported efforts. You can check this list and associated official documentation at https://coreos.com/os/docs/latest/#running-coreos. By far the most common platforms for running CoreOS are these three:

- Amazon Web Services (AWS)
- Internal VM infrastructure (such as OpenStack)
- Bare metal (your own hardware)

Table 4.1 breaks down the costs for each option.

Table 4.1   High-level cost breakdown of common CoreOS platform options

	AWS	Internal VMs	Bare metal
Physical hardware investment		X	X
Personnel to manage host software		X	
Personnel to manage hardware		X	X
Personnel to manage CoreOS	X	X	X
Personnel to manage cloud infrastructure	X		
High initial cost (not including personnel)		X	X
High recurring cost (not including personnel)	X		

Of course, this table is just a guideline; capital expenditures and total cost of ownership (TCO) can be complex topics and are unique for each organization. In my personal experience, it's usually difficult to find personnel. The high recurring cost of AWS is generally offset by needing fewer people and by its ability to get your infrastructure where you want to be much more quickly—a factor you should certainly consider.

In chapter 9, we'll go through a full end-to-end deployment in AWS, using some of the information from this chapter. In addition to being the most likely target platform, AWS's flexibility lets you cover all of CoreOS's features and scenarios without too many caveats regarding your own infrastructure.

4.1.1   *Amazon Web Services*

Infrastructure as a service (IaaS) has gained significant momentum over the last 10 years, and there's no denying that AWS is the market leader in this space. Its biggest competitors are Microsoft Azure and Google Compute Engine (GCE); smaller (but also rapidly growing) competitors include DigitalOcean and Rackspace Cloud. CoreOS supports all of these officially, but we'll primarily discuss IaaS in the context of AWS; most IaaS providers share a lot of the same design patterns, so the examples and language in this chapter should translate easily to any provider with which you have experience.

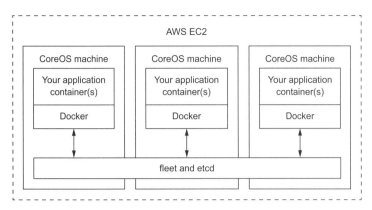

Figure 4.1   AWS deployment with EC2

The biggest difference with AWS is that you have to make an extra decision about your architecture. You can choose to run CoreOS and all your applications on Elastic Compute Cloud (EC2), *or* you can run a controlling CoreOS cluster (such as just fleet and etcd) on EC2 and use Amazon's `ecs-agent` to drive the runtime of your applications in AWS's relatively new Elastic Container Service (ECS). Figure 4.1 illustrates how a cluster looks with just EC2, and figure 4.2 shows it with ECS. Public IaaS providers now have pretty good convergence of features as far as simple compute services go; but AWS is the only one supported by CoreOS that has this abstraction, which can drastically simplify your deployment—you can scale your compute independently of how many CoreOS machines you must manage.

With just EC2 (figure 4.1), the configuration looks a lot like the local workspace you built in chapter 2: three instances, with your application containers running in some configuration on each of the VMs and being controlled with fleet and etcd. Figure 4.2 introduces some interesting abstraction that you may find useful: `ecs-agent`,

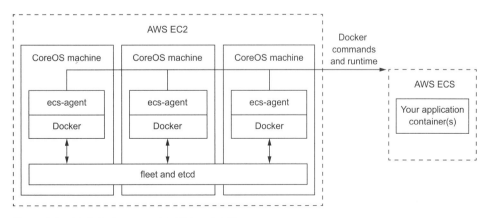

Figure 4.2   AWS deployment with EC2 and ECS

which is officially distributed by Amazon in a Docker container (https://hub.docker .com/r/ amazon/amazon-ecs-agent). It essentially acts as a proxy for all of Docker's commands and runtime, forwarding them into your ECS environment. This means you can have a more attractive separation of concerns between your controllers (your EC2 CoreOS cluster), for which you can now use small instances, and the runtime environment of your applications. fleet and etcd will still run the show, but they can operate independently of ECS's infrastructure. This also means you don't even need to run the CoreOS cluster in EC2, which opens other hybrid approaches: you can have your CoreOS cluster running in your data center, controlling an ECS cluster in AWS.

Chapter 8 will go through detailed examples using both of these models in AWS. Luckily, you don't need to make this choice at the outset. Because `ecs-agent` is transparent to the Docker runtime, you can transition into or out of this model without a huge effort. Either way, for both models, assume for the sake of this section that you're running a CoreOS cluster in AWS EC2.

CoreOS (the company) suggests that you run your machine cluster in EC2 via CloudFormation. If you're unfamiliar with CloudFormation, or if you're new to AWS, check out *Amazon Web Services in Action* by Andreas Wittig and Michael Wittig (Manning, 2015, www.manning.com/books/amazon-web-services-in-action). Briefly, CloudFormation is an AWS system that allows you to write a descriptive manifest of your AWS environment and manage the deployment and changes that occur in that environment. It's a way to record your entire infrastructure and keep it in version control, code review, and so on.

CoreOS provides a basic CloudFormation *template* to get started with CoreOS in EC2, available at https://coreos.com/os/docs/latest/booting-on-ec2.html. It's a great starting point, but keep in mind that it's not sufficient for a robust production deployment, which we'll go through in its entirety later in the book.

4.1.2   *Using in-house VM infrastructure*

You may already have some level of virtualization in your data center that you want to use for the deployment of CoreOS. Currently, CoreOS only officially supports Open-Stack as a target for VM deployment, but the community supports some commonly used products like VMware. Additionally, nothing prevents you from creating CoreOS images for any VM system you're using, although doing so is likely to be time consuming.

> **NOTE**   In my opinion, running CoreOS on a data-center VM platform for production adds little value and a lot of unnecessary complexity. If you already have the hardware, CoreOS is providing the application and infrastructure abstraction for which you'd use virtualization. Running this on top of another abstraction makes it difficult for fleet to understand the topological zones of failure; and because you don't care much about the machine image, the advantages of VM image manipulation aren't useful.

CoreOS on OpenStack uses the common tools `glance` to do image definition and `nova` to initialize the cluster. The official documentation for CoreOS on OpenStack can be found at https://coreos.com/os/docs/latest/booting-on-openstack.html.

4.1.3 *On bare metal*

CoreOS on bare metal (your own data-center hardware) is a great option if you have the engineering resources to manage it and the capacity requirements to make it worthwhile over IaaS. We won't go too much into the economics of this approach, but you'll have to determine where the cost curves meet for IaaS versus bare metal for your organization. Truly massive capacity can see some cost benefits in bare metal over IaaS, if you can afford the time and resources. CoreOS is designed to facilitate that kind of capacity, so it's a great choice if that's your type of environment. You may also have security considerations that forbid the use of IaaS platforms.

CoreOS on your own hardware is officially supported and has some up-front requirements. For simple deployments (such as testing and development), you can use the ISO that CoreOS provides burned onto a CD or thumb drive. This obviously isn't very scalable, so the real requirement for running CoreOS here is running a Pre-boot Execution Environment (PXE) or iPXE server. With this configuration, CoreOS runs entirely in memory. You can optionally install it to disk, but running in memory from PXE yields a high-performance cluster out of the box.

CoreOS on bare metal also likely means the somewhat manual configuration of a network, the specifics of which we'll cover in the next section.

4.2 *Networking considerations*

In all the previous examples in this book, we've assumed that your network for your CoreOS machines is flat and internally open between nodes. This is how a development environment in VirtualBox behaves, but of course this isn't always the case, especially in production environments where you may want to lock things down a little better internally. You have a few options when it comes to configuring networks alongside your CoreOS cluster, some of which are very platform specific (for example, we'll go into how it's done in AWS in chapter 8). Initially, you can refer to figure 4.3 to get an idea of what your CoreOS cluster needs to be functional in terms of port mappings.

Figure 4.3 shows two crucial classes of network configuration you have to do for a CoreOS cluster. First, ports you need to open for administration are (obviously) SSH (TCP/22) and, optionally, the client port for etcd (TCP/2379). Fundamentally, you won't often be `ssh`ing to your nodes directly; but you'll remember from chapter 1 that `fleetctl` can use SSH as a tunnel for executing commands to your cluster remotely. You *can* get away with leaving SSH closed; if you open your etcd client port, `fleetctl` can use the etcd API remotely with the `--driver=API --endpoint=<URI>` flags.

The second critical class of services that need network communications are those that CoreOS (and you!) use to message between machines. You'll also use this internal communication to talk to etcd with `etcdctl` or `curl` in your sidekick services, as you

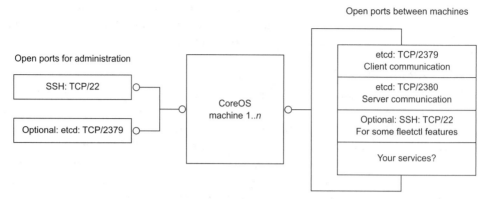

Figure 4.3   CoreOS port mappings

did in examples in chapters 2 and 3. etcd uses TCP/2379 for client communication (etcdctl) and TCP/2380 to internally maintain the cluster configuration. If you want to be able to run fleetctl from one node and have it automatically ssh to the correct node for your command, you'll also have to open SSH (TCP/22) between machines. The legacy ports for etcd are TCP/4001 and TCP/7001. etcd still binds to these ports, too, for backward compatibility, but opening them between machines is entirely optional.

Finally, you also have to decide what ports or ranges of ports to open between machines internally for your application stack. For example, does your Ruby on Rails app need to talk to a Redis instance on another CoreOS machine on port TCP/6379?

The third class of network configuration, which is completely defined by you and your applications (and not shown in figure 4.3) includes the ports and protocols you wish to expose to the world or your customers, or to external firewalls, load balancers, or other networking equipment. Managing this much more dynamic network configuration, as well as the configuration of the networking for your services between machines, is what we'll dive deeply into in this section.

4.2.1   How programmable is your network?

As a simple scenario, let's say you have a PHP application that needs to communicate with MySQL. You can run your PHP app on all machines in your cluster, but MySQL can run on only one machine. You have a security requirement to maintain a default *deny* policy between every machine in your network, but you also want MySQL to be able to run on any *one* machine so that it can move around if there are failures. How can you make your network aware of service changes?

You learned how service sidekick units can announce services on etcd. The same is true in this scenario: your sidekicks should apply some configuration to the networking infrastructure that opens the MySQL port to other machines when it moves. If you're in a public cloud, there are usually well-supported APIs to do this; if you're

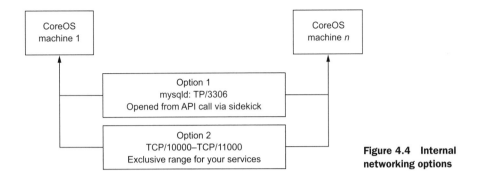

Figure 4.4 Internal networking options

maintaining your own networking equipment, this can be much more difficult or impossible if you can't configure these access control lists (ACLs) programmatically.

There are a couple of options to resolve these problems without an additional system, as shown in figure 4.4 (described in the next subsection):

- *Option 1*—You have an easily programmable network, and you can set this policy with a sidekick.
- *Option 2*—You open a range of ports reserved for internal service mapping.

The other difficulty with automated network configuration internally is that it can become difficult to maintain over time, and you may end up with a lot of complex, opaque configuration in your sidekick unit files. An alternative is to write custom software that uses etcd's ability to have clients listen or poll for changes and apply some network configuration as a result. Obviously, this comes with its own set of complexities and maintenance challenges.

You'll also likely be using some kind of load balancer in front of your CoreOS machines, and this device or service will need a level of programmability. You can initially configure your load balancer to only route requests to a machine based on a health check, or you can use a sidekick service to announce the availability of a service through whatever API your load balancer uses. This is typically less complex and more likely to exist as a feature on load balancers than layer 3 switches, but you'll need to consider your approach (for example, will your service be available if it responds to a port, or does it need to do some bootstrapping?).

4.2.2 *Up and running with flannel*

Flannel is CoreOS's solution to managing a lot of this network complexity within the CoreOS cluster rather than on your networking infrastructure. If you take the same example of a PHP and MySQL app, the connection between the PHP app and MySQL becomes encapsulated and sent over a single port. This way, the MySQL sidekick only needs to tell the PHP app where it is (via etcd), not *both* the application *and* the networking infrastructure.

Flannel creates an overlay network for all of your containers across all the machines in your CoreOS cluster. Flannel encapsulates all this traffic over UDP/8285, which will be the only ACL you have to make between your machines for your own services. Depending on the environment you're in, you can use back ends other than the UDP one: for example, if you're in an AWS VPC, you can use a VPC route table as the back end for flannel. The use of flannel has almost no impact on bandwidth and adds a small penalty to latency.

Let's dive into the example from chapter 3, where you had an NGINX server acting as a load-balancing proxy for Node.js servers, and use the flannel overlay network for communication rather than the VirtualBox network between machines. Refer to figures 4.5 and 4.6 to see the differences in topology (simplified down to just two machines).

Figure 4.5 shows the original network topology of the example in chapter 3. It's a simple internal network

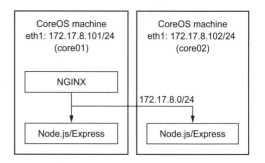

Figure 4.5   Original topology

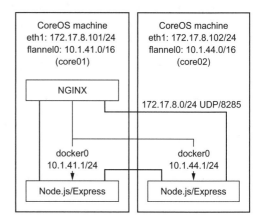

Figure 4.6   Topology with flannel

topology: a shared /24 network between machines. VirtualBox and Vagrant set up an internal network for the cluster in an address space like 172.17.8.0/24 and set up eth1 as an interface for your machines in that subnet. You use that internal network for service discovery and attachment of the NGINX server to the Node.js processes.

As you can see in figure 4.6, a lot more is going on in terms of networking. You still have the same /24 private network between machines, but now its only purpose is to provide an abstraction for flannel, which encapsulates all container traffic over UDP/8285. An internal /16 network on each machine is created on the interface flannel0, and a /24 network is created within that address space for docker0. This keeps traffic between containers running on the same machine efficiently, and it also helps flannel understand the topology.

Back in section 2.1.2, you copied the default Vagrant repo file user-data.sample to user-data. If you look at that file now, you'll see that you already told CoreOS to set up flannel. In the `units:` section, you can see flanneld.service and the 50-network-config.conf file that fires `etcdctl` to set a network for flannel. This is the minimal configuration to get flannel up and running, so if you followed along in chapter 2, you should have everything you need already. `flanneld` should be running, and your Docker containers are already using it.

> **NOTE** You'll use the tool `jq` here: it's a command-line JSON processor, self-described as "`sed` for JSON data." It's included by default in CoreOS, and you can read more about it at https://stedolan.github.io/jq.

Let's look at how you can change some things to use flannel. You won't have to change helloworld-nginx@ or helloworld-nginx-sidekick@ to make this work, just helloworld@ and its sidekick. You still want NGINX to listen on the "real" machine port eth1, because you're considering NGINX to be the edge of this application stack; and because you already have NGINX configured to dynamically change its configuration when the upstream Node.js instances change (see section 3.2.2), you don't have to touch it. You do, of course, have to change helloworld@ (listing 4.1) and helloworld-sidekick@ (listing 4.2).

Listing 4.1   code/ch4/helloworld/helloworld@.service: flannel version

```
[Unit]
Description=Hello World Service
Requires=docker.service
After=docker.service

[Service]
TimeoutStartSec=0
ExecStartPre=-/usr/bin/docker kill helloworld
ExecStartPre=-/usr/bin/docker rm -f helloworld
ExecStartPre=/usr/bin/docker pull mattbailey/helloworld:latest
ExecStart=/usr/bin/docker run --name helloworld mattbailey/helloworld:latest
ExecStartPost=/usr/bin/sh -c 'echo -n FLANNEL_IP= > /run/helloworld.env'
ExecStartPost=/usr/bin/sh -c 'sleep 5; docker inspect helloworld |
   jq -r .[].NetworkSettings.IPAddress >> /run/helloworld.env'
ExecStop=-/usr/bin/docker stop helloworld

[X-Fleet]
Conflicts=helloworld@*
```

Remove the -p 3000:3000 port mapping from the Docker runtime, because you no longer need to open a port to the host interface.

Writes the rest of the environment file, using jq to parse the JSON output of docker inspect helloworld after giving it time to start up

Starts writing an environment file for the sidekick to consume

As you can see, there isn't much to change in the service unit from chapter 3. You're just adding an extra step to provide a little more context to the service (its Docker IP).

Listing 4.2   code/ch4/helloworld/helloworld-sidekick@.service: flannel version

```
[Unit]
Description=Register Hello World %i
BindsTo=helloworld@%i.service
After=helloworld@%i.service
```

```
[Service]
EnvironmentFile=/run/helloworld.env
ExecStartPre=/usr/bin/etcdctl set /services/changed/helloworld 1
ExecStart=/usr/bin/bash -c 'while true; do
    [ "`etcdctl get /services/helloworld/${FLANNEL_IP}`"
    != "server ${FLANNEL_IP}:3000;" ] &&
    etcdctl set /services/changed/helloworld 1;
    etcdctl set /services/helloworld/${FLANNEL_IP}
    \'server ${FLANNEL_IP}:3000;\' --ttl 60;sleep 45;done'
ExecStop=/usr/bin/etcdctl rm /services/helloworld/helloworld@%i
ExecStopPost=/usr/bin/etcdctl set /services/changed/helloworld 1

[X-Fleet]
MachineOf=helloworld@%i.service
```

> **Change the environment file from /etc/environment to the new file the service wrote: /run/helloworld.env.**

> **Uses the new environment variable FLANNEL_IP to set your service discovery keys**

Once you've updated the files, you should be able to destroy your current services and start these updated ones:

```
$ fleetctl destroy helloworld@{1..3}.service \
  helloworld-sidekick@{1..3}.service
$ fleetctl start \
  code/ch4/helloworld/helloworld@{1..3}.service \
  code/ch4/helloworld/helloworld-sidekick@{1..3}.service
```

What does this get you?

- You no longer need to expose a port to the physical interface of your CoreOS machines.
- Your container has internal ownership of a dedicated IP address.
- You don't have to implement port-mapping logic to run the same container on the same machine.
- You can lock down the network between your CoreOS machines.

Now that you have a better understanding of CoreOS networking with fleet, complex application architectures should be much easier to compose, and you can abstract your network configuration out of the docker command being run by your service unit. In some situations, you can also remove the burden of some network configuration from operations and make it easier for the implementers of a service to decide its network configuration in a secure and controllable way. Next, we'll look at the last component of dealing with CoreOS in production: mass storage.

4.3   *Where is your mass storage?*

Mass storage in CoreOS can seem like a mystery. If you're treating individual machines as appliances, you shouldn't care much about their storage. But the reality is that almost all systems eventually need some capacity to manage important data, and how to construct your storage system in a way that doesn't add stateful dependencies to CoreOS may be a little different than how you've done things in the past.

Abstracting mass storage isn't a new concept. People have been doing it in data centers forever—storage area networks (SANs), network-attached storage (NAS), and filesystems like NFS have been in use for a long time. Storage in public clouds is also abstracted, with elastic volumes and services dedicated to storing data as files like AWS S3 or in managed database systems like AWS RDS. But what do you do when you need access to a filesystem shared among machines? This isn't a problem exclusive to CoreOS, of course. Horizontally scaling application stacks that are in some way heavily reliant on local filesystem access is always difficult. There are a few ways to solve this problem and a few factors to consider with respect to your application stack.

4.3.1 *Data systems background*

At the outset, I'd like to point out that, architecturally, relying on a local filesystem for a source of state is generally a bad idea. It's almost *always* better to keep your data in some kind of distributed database that's designed to maintain its own reliability across a cluster of nodes to fit your specific needs. You may have heard of the CAP (consistency, availability, partition tolerance) theorem applied to database systems. In any environment in which you're treating computers as appliances for high horizontal scalability, CoreOS or otherwise, partition tolerance becomes a strong requirement for your data system. Famously, the CAP theorem suggests that you can "choose two of three" (see figure 4.7). This idea can be a little overused and misapplied, but it suggests that these three reliability concepts are more or less impossible to implement simultaneously.

You need partition tolerance, which means you're limited by your application needs when it comes to *other* reliability features you want to use. To achieve high *consistency* with partition tolerance, some operations must be blocking until an operation completes. We can conclude that *availability* suffers in this scenario. To be clear, availability doesn't mean operations fail, but they might have to wait in a queue, which *usually* affects write operations more than read operations. Data systems that guarantee high consistency and high partition tolerance often use the Raft protocol (https://raft .github.io). etcd in CoreOS is an example of a data system that uses Raft; it needs high consistency so you can be sure of the state of your cluster at any point in time.

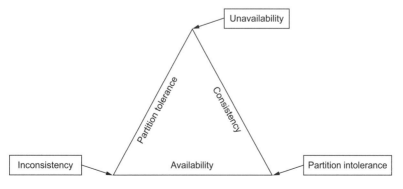

Figure 4.7 CAP theorem: "choose two"

Highly *available* data systems with partition tolerance are also sometimes required. If your application has high-throughput write requirements or doesn't have a strong requirement for data to be *consistent* everywhere in the cluster at the same time, you can use such a data system. These systems typically resolve consistency asynchronously; people often use the term *eventual consistency* to describe them. They frequently align with a Dynamo-like protocol.[1] Examples of Dynamo-like databases are (of course) AWS's DynamoDB, Cassandra, and Riak.

Describing modern data systems could comprise multiple volumes of books, so I won't go into much more depth; but it's important to describe the context in which your data choices will need to be made, and these terms are used throughout this section. In any distributed system, partition tolerance is the *most* important factor in technology choices. We discussed at the end of chapter 3 how greenfield applications are easier to implement in distributed systems than in legacy application stacks, and this is one of the reasons. It can be difficult to migrate a stack that has a data layer that isn't very partition tolerant.

4.3.2   *NAS and storage outsourcing*

The first option for abstracting your persistent filesystems for distribution among nodes is to completely host your filesystems elsewhere. To be clear, this option doesn't include SANs. Although a SAN can be involved at the appropriate layer, we care about the actual filesystem when talking about mass storage in the context of CoreOS, not necessarily how it's attached at the block level. NAS solutions should be pretty familiar to you if you've been in operations for any length of time.

NFS has been the de facto standard NAS protocol for decades. This subsection's title includes "storage outsourcing" for a reason: it's inadvisable to attempt to run NFS on CoreOS as a server. NFS has no facility for sharing its block-level source (which would be completely out of its scope as a service) across nodes, so you're essentially adding another layer of partition *intolerance* by trying to share a filesystem *from* CoreOS. The other direction is fine, however. If you have a reliable NAS that provides NFS or another networked filesystem in your infrastructure, CoreOS as a client of that service is a fine way to add a shared filesystem among nodes. If you go this route, you should be sure to use a system that runs NFSv4, because it has a robust built-in file-locking mechanism to ensure high *consistency*, which is a requirement for using a filesystem.

Various NAS products provide NFSv4. AWS's new (still currently in preview) Elastic File System (EFS) provides NFSv4, and a great many commercial NASs like NetApp serve this protocol as well. The last option for external distributed filesystems is using a user-space filesystem like s3Fs that mounts an S3 bucket as a filesystem. These solutions tend to have pretty poor performance, especially on writes, but they may fit your needs if performance isn't a huge concern.

---

[1] Named after this paper: Giuseppe DeCandia et al., "Dynamo: Amazon's Highly Available Key-value Store," Amazon.com, 2007, http://mng.bz/YY5A.

4.3.3 Ceph

The second option for common access to mass storage is a truly distributed filesystem. There are a few out there, and one of the most popular is Ceph. The Ceph kernel module is officially part of the CoreOS default install and is the only distributed parallel filesystem module included. Setup for Ceph can be nontrivial, but it's a lot less difficult than it was even a year ago. Ceph officially now supports etcd or consul (a system similar to etcd by HashiCorp) as a configuration back end, which makes things significantly easier. A vast array of tunable parameters are provided for Ceph; these are out of scope for this book, but we'll cover some basic usage.

The goal of a Ceph cluster is to unify the storage of several machines in a reliable way. At the end of this example, your Ceph cluster will look like figure 4.8.

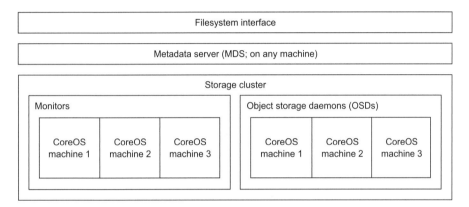

Figure 4.8   Ceph cluster

This figure shows the discrete parts of a Ceph cluster: monitors and object storage daemons (OSDs) run on as many machines in your cluster as you want (although, you should have at least three monitors for a quorum). Together, they make up the *storage cluster* on which the metadata server (MDS) coordinates access and namespacing. The filesystem interface is provided through the `ceph` kernel module. Ceph has some other interfaces available as well, which you can read about at ceph.com.

Let's jump into this example with the development cluster you set up in chapter 2. Before you start running Ceph, you need to attach some more storage to your VMs. You can do this with VirtualBox's command-line utilities:

```
You can choose any path or
filename for your new disks.                        This example uses a
                                                    1,024 MB disk.
$ VBoxManage createhd \
   --filename ceph-disks/ceph-core-01.vdi \
   --size 1024
$ VBoxManage createhd --filename ceph-disks/ceph-core-02.vdi --size 1024
$ VBoxManage createhd --filename ceph-disks/ceph-core-03.vdi --size 1024
```

Now that you have your disks, you need to shut down the cluster, get the VM names, and attach your storage with the following commands:

In the directory where your Vagrant file from chapter 2 is located, make sure your cluster is shut down.

Get the VirtualBox VM names created by Vagrant to attach more storage to them.

```
$ vagrant halt
$ VBoxManage list vms
"vagrant_core-01_1459134252706_21974" {3c944e16-1fcd-4514-b693-98326963a51a}
"vagrant_core-02_1459134273920_21027" {a5bb3429-d9b7-48a7-94ef-99bb05fe1266}
"vagrant_core-03_1459134297702_67743" {71aec75d-aa93-4a6e-b286-f3f2f57a4cf2}
$ VBoxManage storageattach vagrant_core-01_1459134252706_21974 \
  --storagectl 'IDE Controller' --port 1 --device 0 --type hdd \
  --medium ceph-disks/ceph-core-01.vdi
$ VBoxManage storageattach vagrant_core-02_1459134273920_21027 \
  --storagectl 'IDE Controller' --port 1 --device 0 --type hdd \
  --medium ceph-disks/ceph-core-02.vdi
$ VBoxManage storageattach vagrant_core-03_1459134297702_67743 \
  --storagectl 'IDE Controller' --port 1 --device 0 --type hdd \
  --medium ceph-disks/ceph-core-03.vdi
$ vagrant up
```

Start up your cluster again.

Use the VM name with the storageattach command to attach the new disks to each node.

The disks are attached to your VMs; you need to bootstrap one of your nodes with configuration into etcd. ssh into one of your nodes (vagrant ssh core-01, for example), and run the following command:

Currently, this can be etcd or consul (see section 4.3.3).

How the script accesses etcd

```
$ docker run --rm -d --net=host \
  -e KV_TYPE=etcd \
  -e KV_IP=127.0.0.1 \
  -e KV_PORT=4001 \
ceph/daemon:build-master-jewel-ubuntu-14.04 \
  populate_kvstore
```

Uses a specific image to ensure this example works as intended

The ceph/daemon container contains the populate_kvstore script that you'll need to run.

This will exit quickly with a Ceph cluster key (which you don't have to record). If you want to, you can use etcdctl to explore what was written to etcd:

```
core@core-01 ~ $ etcdctl ls /ceph-config/ceph
/ceph-config/ceph/mds
/ceph-config/ceph/auth
/ceph-config/ceph/global
/ceph-config/ceph/mon
/ceph-config/ceph/osd
/ceph-config/ceph/client
```

Show all the keys the populate_kvstore script created

Next, you need to write some unit files to get Ceph up and running; they're shown in listings 4.3, 4.4, and 4.5. Ceph requires three systems: the monitor (mon), the object storage daemon (osd), and the metadata service (mds). You have to run mon and osd on each machine, but you need only one mds (although you can run multiple).

Listing 4.3   code/ch4/ceph/ceph-mon@.service

```
[Unit]
Description=Ceph Monitor
Requires=docker.service
After=docker.service

[Service]
Restart=always
RestartSec=5s
TimeoutStartSec=5
TimeoutStopSec=15
EnvironmentFile=/etc/environment
Environment=CEPH_NETWORK=172.17.8.0/24
Environment=CEPH_NETWORK=172.17.8.0/24
ExecStartPre=-/usr/bin/docker kill %p
ExecStartPre=-/usr/bin/docker rm -f %p
ExecStart=/usr/bin/sh -c "docker run \
  --name %p \
  --rm \
  --net=host \
  -v /var/lib/ceph:/var/lib/ceph \
  -e MON_IP=$COREOS_PUBLIC_IPV4 \
  -e CEPH_PUBLIC_NETWORK=$CEPH_NETWORK \
  -e KV_TYPE=etcd \
  -e KV_IP=127.0.0.1 \
  -e KV_PORT=4001 \
  ceph/daemon:build-master-jewel-ubuntu-14.04 mon"
ExecStop=-/usr/bin/docker stop %p

[X-Fleet]
Conflicts=%p@*
```

Network of your
VirtualBox interfaces

Listing 4.4   code/ch4/ceph/ceph-osd@service

```
[Unit]
Description=Ceph OSD
Requires=docker.service
After=docker.service

[Service]
Restart=always
RestartSec=5s
TimeoutStartSec=10
TimeoutStopSec=15
EnvironmentFile=/etc/environment
ExecStartPre=-/usr/bin/docker kill %p
ExecStartPre=-/usr/bin/docker rm -f %p
ExecStart=/usr/bin/sh -c "docker run \
  --rm \
  --name %p \
  --net=host \
  --privileged=true \
  --pid=host \
  -v /dev/:/dev/ \
  -e OSD_DEVICE=/dev/sdb \
  -e OSD_TYPE=disk \
```

The device that you attached, which
should appear as /dev/sdb in VirtualBox

```
  -e OSD_FORCE_ZAP=1 \                 ⟵
  -e KV_TYPE=etcd \
  -e KV_IP=127.0.0.1 \
  -e KV_PORT=4001 \
  ceph/daemon:build-master-jewel-ubuntu-14.04 osd"
ExecStop=-/usr/bin/docker stop %p

[X-Fleet]
Conflicts=%p@*
```

> Ensures that you clean up the object store, because you're adding a new device. How you manage this in production may be different, so read Ceph's documentation to learn the implications.

Listing 4.5   code/ch4/ceph/ceph-mds.service

```
[Unit]
Description=Ceph Meta Data Service
Requires=docker.service
After=docker.service

[Service]
TimeoutStartSec=0
EnvironmentFile=/etc/environment
ExecStartPre=-/usr/bin/docker kill %p
ExecStartPre=-/usr/bin/docker rm -f %p
ExecStartPre=/usr/bin/docker pull ceph/daemon
ExecStart=/usr/bin/sh -c "docker run \
  --rm \
  --name %p \
  --net=host \
  -e CEPHFS_CREATE=1 \                 ⟵
  -e KV_TYPE=etcd \
  -e KV_IP=127.0.0.1 \
  -e KV_PORT=4001 \
ceph/daemon:build-master-jewel-ubuntu-14.04 mds"
ExecStop=-/usr/bin/docker stop %p

[X-Fleet]
Conflicts=ceph-mds@*
```

> Makes sure you're creating a new filesystem on Ceph for this example

Let's get these files up and running on your machines with `fleetctl`:

```
$ fleetctl start \
    code/ch4/ceph/ceph-mon@{1..3}.service \
    code/ch4/ceph/ceph-osd@{1..3}.service \
    code/ch4/ceph/ceph-mds.service
```

You now have Ceph distributing a filesystem across your cluster. You can optionally use Ceph's S3 API work-alike called RADOS to provide a distributed S3 interface to this data, or you can mount it directly in CoreOS:

> Ceph uses some authentication; the admin key is written in etcd.

```
$ sudo mount -t ceph 72.17.8.101:/ /media -o
 ➥name=admin,secret=$(etcdctl get /ceph-config/ceph/adminKeyring
 ➥| grep key | cut -d' ' -f3)               ⟵
$ df -h
172.17.8.101:/   45G  100M   45G   1% /media   ⟵
```

> Out of three 20 GB volumes, you've lost a total of 15 GB to replication.

This is only a basic example of how to get Ceph up and running as a solution to distributing stateful data across your cluster on a filesystem. Ceph is a complex system and could fill a book by itself; this should get you started, but your exact implementation will have a lot of unique details. If you're planning to (or must) use Ceph, reading the documentation available at ceph.com is crucial.

At the end of the day, you must determine the right kind of storage mechanism for you and your organization. Ceph can be difficult to support. If you're already in AWS, using AWS EFS (although still currently in preview at the time of this writing) is probably a better bet for solving your problems around distributed storage and relieving you of this kind of burden. But Ceph will remain a leader in this space; the company was recently acquired by Red Hat, Inc., so the tooling and documentation should continue to improve.

4.4   Summary

- CoreOS officially supports some of the most popular IaaS platforms: AWS, GCE, DigitalOcean, and Rackspace Cloud.
- CoreOS officially only supports OpenStack, but there is community support for VMware.
- Bare-metal deployments are officially supported via iPXE.
- CoreOS clusters expect communication between its essential services (etcd and fleet) and, optionally, your own services.
- You can use flannel to abstract network configuration into software with minimal overhead and performant, pluggable back ends.
- Your choice of database system can affect various aspects of reliability in CoreOS.
- Mass object storage can be a challenge when you're porting legacy applications that rely on filesystems.
- You can provide distributed filesystems either via external components (NAS or AWS EFS) or internally via Ceph.

Application architecture and workflow

At this point, you should have a basic, practical understanding of how CoreOS functions. This chapter is intended as a primer for someone with a role like software or systems architect. The assumption is that you'll be building a new application for, or migrating an existing application to, CoreOS. As such, this chapter is less about technical practice and more about the planning you need to do before any technical implementation.

5.1 Your application and the twelve-factor methodology

Suppose you've been tasked with drafting the architecture for a new SaaS product, and you want to use CoreOS as your target platform. Where do you start? What are the best practices in this space? Although it isn't explicitly meant for CoreOS, the *twelve-factor methodology* (http://12factor.net) is a set of guidelines for successfully architecting complex application stacks. This approach doesn't define any technologies or processes but is specifically useful in one of two ways, depending on your starting point:

- If you're building an application from scratch, it can guide your choices of technology and workflows.
- If you're migrating or figuring out how to scale an existing application, it can show you where and how those tasks will be difficult.

Briefly, the 12 factors are as follows:

- *Codebase*—Your application's code exists in source control, from which you do many deploys.
- *Dependencies*—Supporting libraries should be explicit and isolated.
- *Config*—The application configuration should be per environment.
- *Backing services*—Data, persistence, and external services are all abstracted.
- *Build, release, run*—The codebase is deployed through these strictly separated steps.
- *Processes*—Your application process(es) should be stateless and share nothing.
- *Port binding*—The application should be able to bind its own service.
- *Concurrency*—Scale is achieved by adding processes (a.k.a. *horizontal scaling*).
- *Disposability*—Processes should be disposable and have quick startup.
- *Development/production parity*—Your development environment should be as similar to production as possible.
- *Logs*—Logs should act as event streams and exist in the application as unbuffered writes to stdout.
- *Admin processes*—Management tools should be task-oriented one-offs.

Throughout this chapter, I'll refer to these factors when they come into play for architecting an application for CoreOS. Some have less relevance than others with respect to CoreOS, and it's always up to you whether you want to implement this methodology into your organization's technical design process. CoreOS's design resolves many of these factors for you, so we'll start by going over each of them and where CoreOS does (or doesn't) help you.

5.1.1 CoreOS's approach

You're reading this book, so I'm sure it's no surprise that abstractions are how we maintain sanity in complex systems. You've probably experienced that it can be hard to find agreement on where those abstractions should be, how they function, and how to use them. Even at the level most relevant to CoreOS, best practice is still an open question: virtualization and containerization have overlaps and competing technologies internally. Obviously, with CoreOS, you've made a choice to go with containerization over virtualization to abstract your services; you've chosen to rely on etcd and fleet to manage at least some of your configuration state and scheduling for scale. With CoreOS, you can also manage stateful data services at scale, and you have a networking abstraction system through flannel.

If these seem like opinionated systems, that's because they are, by design. Orchestrated together, they're designed to immediately solve some of the twelve-factor problems.

CODEBASE

CoreOS doesn't provide much here. As long as your final product consists of a container and service units, the codebase and source control you use are inconsequential. This is, of course, by design: the fundamentals of containerization provide an explicitly generic platform so you aren't tied to any one technology. You *will*, however, have to consider your CoreOS deployment *in* your codebase; section 5.2 goes into the details of what this means.

DEPENDENCIES

Nothing is explicitly gained by using CoreOS for this factor, other than the inherent dependency isolation you achieve by using containers. So, you'll likely apply this factor implicitly.

CONFIG

This factor ensures that your software's configuration is relative to its environment. This means *not* baking your configuration parameters into a build, and making sure that what needs to be changed in the config is available via environment variables. CoreOS solves this problem at scale with etcd, which gives you a distributed store specifically designed for managing environment configuration.

BACKING SERVICES

This factor has more to do with ensuring that services that back your application (like a database) are interchangeable. CoreOS doesn't enforce or solve this problem explicitly but does make it easier to solve by better defining the dynamic configuration, as per the third factor. And by using containers, you probably already have loose coupling between services.

BUILD, RELEASE, RUN

The build and release processes are out of the scope of what CoreOS can help with. But fleet and its version of systemd provide the standard for application runtime, and containerization implicitly provides some level of release context (such as Docker tags).

PROCESSES

CoreOS resolves process isolation with containerization. It also *enforces* that isolation by requiring you to build your containers with the expectation that they could lose state.

PORT BINDING

Port binding is well covered in CoreOS. Containerization and flannel give you the tools to abstract and control the port binding of your applications.

CONCURRENCY

With fleet, CoreOS gives you a number of tools to control concurrency among your service units. Flannel also helps you keep the port configuration consistent across multiple instances of the same process.

DISPOSABILITY

CoreOS strictly enforces disposability. You must rely on fleet and etcd as the central sources of truth for your architecture's state.

DEVELOPMENT/PRODUCTION PARITY

This is a goal achieved by containerization, but not by CoreOS specifically.

LOGS

CoreOS expects all containers to output only to stdout and stderr. It controls this stream with systemd's journal and provides access to it via fleet.

ADMIN PROCESSES

CoreOS doesn't facilitate creating administrative tools in any way, but it does provide an interface via fleet and etcd to make creating those tools easier.

As you design your application architecture, keep in mind these 12 factors and how CoreOS augments their application. Remember, too, that these are just guidelines: especially if you're migrating an application that has any components that don't fit the model, those components can be difficult or impossible to transform into an optimal configuration.

5.1.2 *The architecture checklist*

To locate the holes in your architecture, learn how to begin writing your technical design, and determine how far you are from an optimal twelve-factor configuration, it's useful to start with a checklist:

- What infrastructure are you using for CoreOS?
- Which services are stateful, and which are stateless?
- Are dependencies between services clear and documented?
- Is the configuration that will describe those dependencies well known, and can you apply that model in etcd?
- What does your process model look like?
- What services and configuration of your system do you need to expose outside of the cluster?

If you can answer all these questions in detail with information from this chapter and chapter 4, you'll be well prepared for building out a complex system in CoreOS. Before you start applying your architecture, though, you need to address some requirements in your application code.

5.2   *The software development cycle*

You've gone through the process of mapping out the technical design for your latest project with the twelve-factor methodology in mind, including everything CoreOS brings to the table. What details need to be resolved in your various codebases to make this design fully functional?

Your codebase, dependency management, and build/release/run workflows are all part of a software development lifecycle that may or may not be well defined in your organization. Determining how you'll build around or fit CoreOS into that cycle is, of course, critical to your success. We won't go into how Docker solves some of these problems; for more detail on the benefits of containers, *Docker in Action* (Nickoloff, 2016, www.manning.com/books/docker-in-action) is a good resource. Specifically, though, we'll cover where the CoreOS-related components live in your codebase, how that code resolves dependencies between services, and how to automate the deployment of your services. This will mostly be a high-level discussion: the actual implementation will be very specific to your application and your organization. Once you've mapped out all these components, you'll be ready to create a development and test plan for getting your application live.

5.2.1   *Codebase and dependencies*

In this book, you've seen a lot of custom scripts and logic being built to hook into CoreOS's various features and systems. You absolutely should retain your unit files in source control. Where you do that starts to become a bit tricky. Unless you're deploying a single monolithic application with no outside dependencies, you'll have services that are shared. Often these are persistence layers, which probably exist somewhat outside of your development cycle. You also may be using a mix of containers that are publicly available images (for example, official Docker Hub library containers), containers that are based on public images, and some that are entirely built from scratch. Keeping the latter two types in the source control of their respective projects is easy, but containers you're using straight from the public Docker library need to have their service unit files in source control as well.

The unit files for public images probably contain *more* logic than your custom ones, because custom applications are more likely to have environmental clustering logic built in than a base Docker image is. We'll look more at what that means in the next subsection. If you're using Git, my recommendation is to maintain a repository for your units with Git submodules in your custom applications. Taking a peek at chapter 6, the file tree looks something like the following.

> **NOTE** It's a good idea to begin getting familiar with the layout of the project you start in chapter 6. You'll build on it throughout the rest of the book.

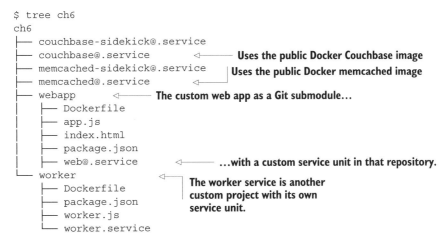

Keeping a layout like this serves a few purposes:

- You can keep an eye on the big picture of the layout of your applications.
- There's a clear separation between custom code and publicly available services.
- You can use this repository with its submodules as a template for big-picture, continuous integration.
- Service dependencies become more obvious.

The last point is especially important: easily understanding how the different parts of your project depend on one another is a great benefit in an organization where there are many engineers. Understanding the layout at a glance makes this simple. For example, if worker also depended on webapp, I probably would have made it a Git submodule of webapp. But wait! What if I create a new service that depends on both webapp and worker? The short answer is, don't! Doing so would break the processes factor in the twelve-factor model as well as, arguably, dependencies. We'll go into microservices a bit in the next section; but having a service with dependencies on multiple other services should be a big red flag that you're creating very tight coupling between services, which can exponentially compound complexity and add corner cases of cascading application failures that may be difficult to predict. If you need to do so and still want to maintain this kind of file tree, you can either duplicate the submodule or symlink one to the other.

This brings us to environment logic and microservice interactions, which will become important to your development cycle when you're building services based on infrastructure as code.

5.2.2 *Environment logic and microservices*

CoreOS is a platform that relies on your ability to build some kind of logic around the way it expresses the state of the cluster via etcd. You've seen a lot of examples in this book with sidekicks that react to or change this state in some way. This kind of logic can get a little complex in Bash, not to mention being difficult to maintain over time.

It's sometimes useful to be able to write things like sidekicks and functions in your applications that respond or write to this state. Usually, you can gather more context about your application from within its runtime, which opens up other opportunities in your app to communicate its status with (and use information from) etcd.

There are libraries for etcd in many different programming languages; if your language of choice doesn't have a library, you can always fall back on the simple HTTP REST interface. Before we dive into using these APIs, let's talk about the process model. Many projects and tools are designed to add a second layer of supervision to your processes; a good example is PM2 for Node.js applications (well, PM2 can launch any kind of process). There are plenty of good reasons to use these kinds of systems: for example, they can provide additional monitoring and performance-reporting metrics. But let's look at what this looks like in practice in a process tree:

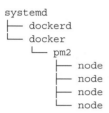

```
systemd
├── dockerd
└── docker
    └── pm2
        ├── node
        ├── node
        ├── node
        └── node
```

Although this isn't explicitly stated in the twelve-factor model, it's useful to try to think about your applications in the context of the scheduler they're running under, and to understand them as dependencies with their own state. The node processes depend on pm2, and pm2 depends on docker, which loosely depends on dockerd. systemd is left not knowing the state of the node processes; essentially, you're relying on a second process scheduler. It's debatable whether the benefits of whatever this second scheduler does outweigh the context lost to the system scheduler, but it's certainly *less complex* if only one scheduler is determining how things are run.

Why is this important? If you're following a microservices model, this begins to go against the isolation of processes that gives you the benefits of loosely coupled systems. It also means you can't easily derive state from the exit code of the node process in this example. If you have small services doing discrete things, it's convenient to exit the program with an exit code that gives context to the scheduler to know whether it should be restarted. For example, if only *one* of the node processes throws an exception and exits, should they all fail? Or will they fail one by one and be restarted by pm2, and systemd will never be aware of the context?

You'll see how to use this in the next chapter. In the web service application, logic checks etcd for a set operation on an etcd key set by Couchbase (the database used in the next chapter). If it sees this operation, it will exit(0), which lets systemd know it should be restarted—because that means Couchbase has moved to a different machine. In a microservices architecture, where things are loosely coupled and startup time is trivial for processes, exiting processes is usually the best way to reestablish state. This pattern also adheres well to considering the initial state immutable rather than something that's copied and changed in the service.

I could fill many books with discussions of process architectures and state immutability. Ultimately, the implementation is up to you. How strictly you want to follow these models may or may not be up to you as an implementer of services on CoreOS, but you should be aware of how those choices affect the complexity of the overall system.

5.2.3 *The application edge*

The last consideration for a successful deployment is something that falls a bit out of scope for this book: how to expose the edge of your application to the world. This will be specific to your application, your organization, and your chosen platform for your infrastructure.

The last item on the checklist should cover the "what" of the items you need to expose, and the construction of that component probably is coupled fairly tightly to what you choose for your edge. Load balancers, DNS, external logging and alerting systems, policies and reporting, and backup/recovery procedures are all part of the edge of your system as a whole. They may be completely separate systems that you can deploy with CoreOS in and of themselves. Deciding how this hierarchy works is usually a larger organizational question (enterprise architecture), but you'll want to be sure that these top-level components have separate zones of failure and scale vectors from the stack you're responsible for deploying.

5.3 *Summary*

- Apply the twelve-factor model to your application stack, where possible.
- Make a high-level checklist for your architecture, starting with the one included in section 5.1.2.
- Have a clear mapping of dependencies between services.
- The application edge is the ultimate goal. It's often useful to work on the architecture design both from the internal application requirements and from the outside expectation of the product.

Web stack
application example

This chapter covers

- Deploying a multitier web application to a CoreOS cluster
- Applying autodiscovery systems in application logic and service unit files
- Testing failover of discrete layers

In this chapter, you'll begin fleshing out a full application stack on CoreOS. This isn't an application development book, so the example is a bit contrived, but it's similar to any complex stack you might see that contains a number of different services with different purposes. This example will develop the information you've already learned about CoreOS into a more real-world scenario. The application you'll build and deploy will be iterated on throughout the rest of the book, just as you'd expect in the real world.

6.1   *Scope of the example*

This example will cover the setup of a full-stack web application with the following components:

- Node.js back end (app.js) running
- Express HTTP server
- Socket.IO WebSocket server
- Node.js worker process for data acquisition (worker.js)
- Memcached for the `express-session` store
- Couchbase as the persistent database
- React for front-end view composition

By the end of this chapter, your infrastructure on CoreOS will look like figure 6.1. You'll have an instance of your web application (app.js) and a memcached service running on all three machines, as well as one Couchbase instance and one instance of your data-acquisition program (worker.js).

This is intentionally a fairly complex application to set up, and it's worth going into a little detail about why I chose these components. First, avoiding what are known as *full-stack MVC frameworks* like Ruby on Rails, MEAN.io, Meteor, and so on was a conscious choice—not because I think they're bad in any way, but because there are quite a few well-written and *scripted* guides for getting those frameworks running in CoreOS. This is fantastic, but it leaves how the components interact with each other via CoreOS a black box. The purpose of this book is to give you the tools to be successful in operating anything in CoreOS, because even if you're using a popular stack with a community of people forming best practices for deploying to CoreOS, you don't want to get stuck when someone adds a new component that doesn't fit in. As I'm sure you know, in the real world, components are added or changed for different features.

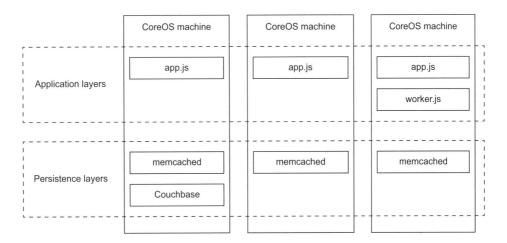

Figure 6.1   Infrastructure of the example

A small caveat about Couchbase: this chapter won't cover a high-availability (HA), fault-tolerant deployment for Couchbase. You'll deploy it in such a way that it won't cause downtime for this application, but you won't persist the data after the application is shut down. In chapter 7, you'll expand on your knowledge from this chapter and build out the Couchbase cluster for HA and fault tolerance when you extend the example to cover a Big Data application example.

Comment on learning

In college, I took an anthropology course in linguistics. In this course, we had to learn a system called the International Phonetic Alphabet (IPA), which is a system of symbols that represent all the sounds made by people's mouths. The exams involved the professor reciting a speech and us transcribing it in IPA. But the professor never gave these exams in English, because it's more difficult to transcribe into IPA a language you already know: you end up parsing the information and not listening to the sounds.

The same concept applies here: these components aren't part of any well-known full-stack system as a whole, even though they may be well known individually. The focus is on how the building blocks connect, not on how to move an entire building.

6.1.1   *What does this app do?*

The purpose of this application is to aggregate some information from Meetup.com's public WebSocket API, store it in Couchbase asynchronously, and serve it back up with a high-availability web service via WebSockets. You're also going to store sessions with memcached. In short, the app collects, stores, and displays data, all while taking advantage of CoreOS's features for scalability and availability. You'll need the following:

- Memcached instances you can scale horizontally
- A Couchbase node to store your critical data
- A single worker process to store data from Meetup.com
- The Express and Socket.IO Node.js app that you can scale horizontally

The express-connect sessions don't serve any functional purpose in the example other than adding a common component that relies on an ephemeral state mechanism (memcached). Everything else is functionally designed to build this application stack, which looks like any kind of web application designed to aggregate and display information for a user. The example uses Meetup.com's stream because it's a convenient, publicly available WebSocket API that has a lot of chatter so you can see it working. You can read more about it at http://mng.bz/pEai, but those details aren't particularly important to this example.

Everything that's custom in this app is written in JavaScript. I've chosen this for a few reasons:

- JS is arguably *the* most popular language right now, and most readers probably have some familiarity with it.

- The syntax is terse enough that I don't have to make you read/copy pages of code.
- There's a ton of boilerplate you won't have to write.
- There's a high likelihood that you'll encounter a requirement to deploy a Node.js application in the real world.
- I know JS pretty well.

All that being said, JavaScript knowledge isn't a prerequisite for readers of this book, and you'll see annotations throughout this example that explain what's important as takeaways for the applications in the context of CoreOS deployment, and also what *isn't* important. One thing that *is* important is what this architecture looks like, so you understand what you're deploying.

6.1.2   *App architecture overview*

Figure 6.2 shows how this application is put together. It should be simple enough to understand what's going on between all the components, but complex enough to be an interesting exercise in deployment that covers a lot of common patterns.

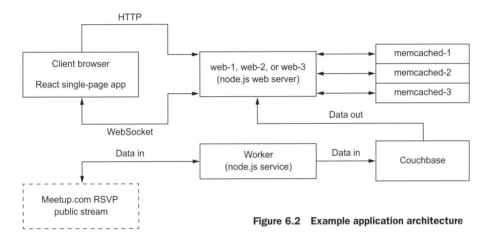

Figure 6.2   Example application architecture

THE MEMCACHED "CLUSTER"

Memcached doesn't really "cluster" in any sense other than that you'll be running a bunch of memcached processes. The nodes don't need to know about each other, and the processes don't write to disk. The connect-memcached back-end library for express-connect (the session library) just needs to know where all the memcached nodes are. The library uses an internal hash to know where to find data (you don't have to worry about any of that). You'll know express-connect is working if you get a cookie when you visit the app in a browser.

THE COUCHBASE SERVER

Couchbase is a little more involved in the setup. As I mentioned earlier, you won't be persisting the data (yet), but you'll have to do some setup automation so that you can connect to your Couchbase server easily. Couchbase is a document store with robust clustering capabilities; we'll spend a lot more time in chapter 7 focusing on a custom data-system deployment that uses it. For now, accept this HA "hole" in this deployment for the sake of staying focused. Couchbase is overkill for this application, but it's a good example to get started with, and its API is fairly easy to use.

THE WORKER

Many applications rely on an asynchronous worker to perform some task: in this case, data aggregation. Like many APIs, Meetup's RSVP WebSocket will rate-limit you if you try to make too many connections to it. Assuming your network is behind some kind of NAT, this means you'll need no more than one worker to gather this data; the API allows only one connection from an IP. Because it's a WebSocket, you don't gain anything from having multiple workers gathering that data anyway. This is a great use case for CoreOS, because once you get your service running, you don't care which node it's running on; and it should require no state other than how to connect to Couchbase, so it can be completely ephemeral.

THE WEB APP

You'll be using a combination of Express.js (a popular Node.js web framework) and Socket.IO (a popular WebSocket implementation in Node.js) to serve your application. Express will handle the session with memcached as its session store and will serve up the index.html file. In index.html is some very basic JavaScript to listen to the `socket.io` WebSocket and update the page when a message is sent.

The app contains an interval loop that fetches a view from Couchbase and sends a message via Socket.IO to any clients listening. Socket.IO has the ability to react to WebSocket events on the same port on which Express is serving HTTP, so you only need to worry about one port being exposed.

6.1.3 *The target environment*

Not surprisingly, you'll use a Vagrant cluster of three nodes to go through this example. We'll approach each of these components individually, but we'll start with Couchbase because it may require some low-level changes to your Vagrant development cluster.

This architecture is a fairly common kind of layered web application you've likely seen before. When you're building out a system in CoreOS, these are the kinds of details you'll need to gather about the application in order to deploy it effectively. Jumping into persistence layers next, you'll see how to begin applying the architecture.

6.2 Setting up persistence layers

You have two persistence layers (see figure 6.3) that represent state in the application: Couchbase and memcached. As explained, in this example, both of these are somewhat ephemeral, but you'll use Couchbase as if it weren't.

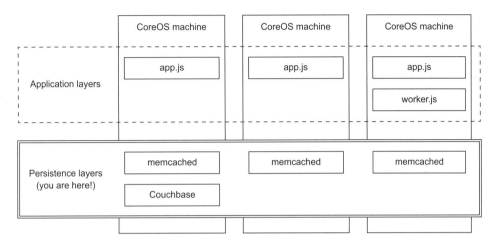

Figure 6.3   Persistence layers

When building out complex application stacks, especially in development, it's a good plan of attack to start with the persistence layer, because it's usually the only component you can't wipe completely if you mess up. The other reason you're starting with Couchbase is that you may have to rebuild your Vagrant cluster if you didn't provision your instances with at least 1.5 GB of RAM. If you didn't make this modification in chapter 2, you can go back and look at how to change the RAM for your VMs, but the quick version is as follows (config.rb in your vagrant directory):

Assigns 2 GB per VM.
You'll need at least 1.5 GB.

```
# Edit config.rb
so that you have this line:
//$vm_memory = 2048
$vm_cpus = 1
$ vagrant destroy -f
...
$ vagrant up
...
```

You can bump this to two cores per VM if you have the resources, but doing so isn't required.

Deletes your VMs

Re-creates your VMs

> **NOTE** If you're using `fleetctl` from your host workstation with the SSH tunnel, creating new VMs creates a new SSH host key, so you'll have to delete the one in $HOME/.fleetctl/known_hosts.

Once you're back up, you can move on to getting Couchbase initialized and running.

6.2.1   Couchbase setup

Now that your Vagrant cluster is ready, it's time to set up Couchbase. First, you need to create a new service-unit template.

Listing 6.1   code/ch6/couchbase@.service

For now, cleans up data on exit

Gives a 20-second restart buffer because Couchbase can take some time to cleanly shut down and start

ulimit specifically needed for Couchbase. You can read more about what these do in the Docker documentation.

You want Couchbase to restart for any reason.

Optional: opens a web admin panel for Couchbase to the host IP

```
[Unit]
Description=Couchbase Service %i
Requires=flanneld.service
After=flanneld.service

[Service]
TimeoutSec=0
Restart=always
RestartSec=20
ExecStartPre=-/usr/bin/docker kill couchbase-%i
ExecStartPre=/usr/bin/docker pull couchbase:community-4.0.0
ExecStartPre=-/usr/bin/docker rm -f couchbase-%i
ExecStart=/usr/bin/docker run \
    --rm \
    -p 8091:8091 \
    --name couchbase-%i \
    --ulimit nofile=40960:40960 \
    couchbase:community-4.0.0
ExecStartPost=/usr/bin/bash -c 'sleep 5; \
    FLANNELIP=`docker inspect couchbase-%i | jq -r .[].NetworkSettings.IPAddress`; \
    echo "Started on $FLANNELIP"; sleep 2; \
    until docker run --rm couchbase:community-4.0.0 \
        couchbase-cli \
        cluster-init \
        -c $FLANNELIP:8091 \
        --cluster-username=Administrator \
        --cluster-password=Password1 \
        --services=data,index,query \
        --cluster-ramsize=500; \
```

Loops until this succeeds: sets up the server's initial configuration

Same line used in chapter 4 when we discussed using flannel to get the internal IP

Sets the initial cluster password. You can choose whatever you want, but this is for administration, not connecting. You'll use this again in chapter 7.

Official Couchbase Community Edition image

```
  do echo "Retrying init..."; sleep 2; done \
  docker run --rm couchbase:community-4.0.0 \
    couchbase-cli \
    bucket-create \
    -c $FLANNELIP:8091 \
    -u Administrator \
    -p Password1 \
    --bucket=default \
    --bucket-type=couchbase \
    --bucket-ramsize=500 \
    --bucket-replica=1 \
    --cluster-ramsize=500'
ExecStop=-/usr/bin/docker kill --signal=SIGTERM couchbase-%i
```

Sets up an initial bucket, which is the top-level Couchbase namespace for you to use

Notice that you do quite a bit of initialization with magic numbers and strings. Later in this chapter, we'll talk about adding more configuration abstraction to the project as a whole. Next, here's the sidekick for the service.

Listing 6.2   code/ch6/couchbase-sidekick@.service

```
[Unit]
Description=Couchbase Service Sidekick %i
BindsTo=couchbase@%i.service
After=couchbase@%i.service

[Service]
TimeoutStartSec=0
RestartSec=1
Restart=always
ExecStartPre=-/usr/bin/etcdctl rm /services/couchbase/%i
ExecStart=/usr/bin/bash -c ' \
  while true; do \
    sleep 5; \
    FLANNELIP=`docker inspect couchbase-%i
      | jq -r .[].NetworkSettings.IPAddress`; \
    etcdctl update --ttl 8 /services/couchbase/%i $FLANNELIP || \
    etcdctl set --ttl 8 /services/couchbase/%i $FLANNELIP; \
  done'
ExecStop=-/usr/bin/etcdctl rm /services/couchbase/%i'

[X-Fleet]
MachineOf=couchbase@%i.service
```

Makes sure you start with a clean slate, in case this service switched hosts too quickly for the TTL

Updates this value if it exists, or sets it if it doesn't, with a TTL of 8 seconds

Explicitly cleans up if you Stop

This mostly looks like previous sidekick units you've seen, with one difference: you use logic to either update or set the etcd key. This distinction is important, and the logic works like this: if you're refreshing the key so it doesn't expire, you want to fire an update event; but if this is a new location for the node, you want to fire a set event. Later in this chapter, when we look at the application, you'll see that you restart the web service on set but not on update, so you're not restarting the app every 5 seconds.

Now let's get Couchbase and the sidekick running:

```
$ fleetctl start code/ch6/couchbase@1.service code/ch6/couchbase-
    sidekick@1.service
```

After waiting a few seconds, you should be able to look at the Couchbase admin console on http://172.17.8.101:8091 and log in with "Administrator" and "Password1". Notice that you start only *one* instance of Couchbase with the template. (You didn't have to make this a template, but you'll build on this example in the following chapter when you take this install and make it high availability.) Next, let's move on to the other piece of state: memcached.

> **NOTE** Couchbase may start on a different machine, so you can either check with `fleetctl  list-units` or try http://172.17.8.102:8091 or http://172.17.8.103:8091.

6.2.2 *Setting up memcached*

Setting up memcached is simple and follows a pattern similar to Couchbase, except that you don't need to deal with any bootstrapping or login information. As with Couchbase, you also need a main unit template (listing 6.3) and a sidekick (listing 6.4). *Unlike* Couchbase, you can (and should) start more than one instance.

Listing 6.3   code/ch6/memcached@.service

```
[Unit]
Description=Memcached Instance %i
Requires=flanneld.service
After=flanneld.service

[Service]
TimeoutStartSec=0
RestartSec=1
Restart=always
ExecStartPre=-/usr/bin/docker rm -f memcached-%i
ExecStartPre=/usr/bin/docker pull memcached:1
ExecStart=/usr/bin/docker run --rm --name memcached-%i memcached:1
ExecStop=-/usr/bin/docker rm -f memcached-%i
```

Makes sure you start from scratch

Official memcached Docker image

This should look pretty familiar by now: it's a simple service template that also cleans up after itself. Now you'll make an equally familiar sidekick.

Listing 6.4   code/ch6/memcached-sidekick@.service

```
[Unit]
Description=Register memcached %i
BindsTo=memcached@%i.service
After=memcached@%i.service

[Service]
TimeoutStartSec=0
RestartSec=1
Restart=always
ExecStartPre=-/usr/bin/etcdctl rm /services/memcached/%i
ExecStart=/usr/bin/bash -c ' \
  while true; do \
    sleep 5; \
```

```
    FLANNELIP=`docker inspect memcached-%i | jq -
      r .[].NetworkSettings.IPAddress`; \
    etcdctl update --ttl 8 /services/memcached/%i $FLANNELIP || \
    etcdctl set --ttl 8 /services/memcached/%i $FLANNELIP; \
  done'
ExecStop=-/usr/bin/etcdctl rm /services/memcached/%i'

[X-Fleet]
MachineOf=memcached@%i.service
```

Much like the Couchbase sidekick, you grab the flannel IP, update or set it to a key in etcd with a TTL of 8 seconds, and attach it to the memcached unit. You can run as many of these as you want.

Notice that you did *not* give a `Conflicts=` line for memcached. Because you're using flannel, you can run multiple instances of memcached without having to step on ports, because the instances will be running on their own IPs within the flannel network. Go ahead and start the memcached cluster and sidekick:

```
$ fleetctl start \
    code/ch6/memcached@{1..3}.service \
    code/ch6/memcached-sidekick@{1..3}.service
...
```

With all these systems running, you can verify that things look good with `fleetctl list-units` as usual, and check your etcd keys to make sure everything was set correctly:

```
$ fleetctl list-units
UNIT                        MACHINE                 ACTIVE      SUB
couchbase-sidekick@1.service    72476ea6.../172.17.8.101    active    running
couchbase@1.service             72476ea6.../172.17.8.101    active    running
memcached-sidekick@1.service    ac6b3188.../172.17.8.101    active    running
memcached-sidekick@2.service    b598f557.../172.17.8.102    active    running
memcached-sidekick@3.service    ac6b3188.../172.17.8.103    active    running
memcached@1.service             ac6b3188.../172.17.8.101    active    running
memcached@2.service             b598f557.../172.17.8.102    active    running
memcached@3.service             ac6b3188.../172.17.8.103    active    running
$ etcdctl ls --recursive /services
/services/couchbase
/services/couchbase/1
/services/memcached
/services/memcached/3
/services/memcached/1
/services/memcached/2
$ etcdctl get /services/memcached/1
10.1.35.2
$ etcdctl get /services/couchbase/1
10.1.1.2
```

Next, let's move on to setting up the custom software application.

6.3   *Application layer*

The application for this example has two parts (see figure 6.4):

- A worker you'll run only one of, which will watch the Meetup WebSocket for any changes and write them to the Couchbase document store
- A cluster of many web servers running the custom back-end HTTP service with Express

You'll follow a single-process model for the web service, so each container will spawn only one Node.js process. It's possible to spawn multiple Node.js processes, but that's beyond the scope of this book. You do have the ability to spawn many within the same container, or you can spawn one per container and add another load-balancer layer (for example, with HAProxy) on each machine.

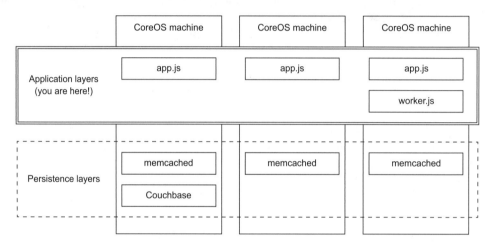

Figure 6.4   Application layers

Earlier in the book, I mentioned that you have a choice when it comes to interacting with etcd: you can do most of the interactions from your unit file; or your application can communicate with etcd, which opens up a little more programmability for what you're trying to accomplish that might be painful in Bash. Because you're deploying custom software here, this example provides an opportunity to show that approach; so your unit files will be simple, and the complexity of interacting with etcd will be built into the application.

6.3.1   *The worker*

The worker pattern is common in software development today, especially in any system that either processes or aggregates data in quantity. Anything that isn't needed for real-time consumption by a user and that you can do asynchronously can use a worker.

By the end of this section, you'll see your data start to populate the Couchbase server you've set up (see figure 6.5). In this case, the worker gathers data from a Web-Socket that emits RSVPs provided by Meetup.com and dumps the data into Couch-base. You might want to do this because you can't query Meetup.com's historical RSVPs and can only consume them in real time; so this is essentially archiving that stream as it emits events. Let's begin with the service unit file, because it's extremely simple.

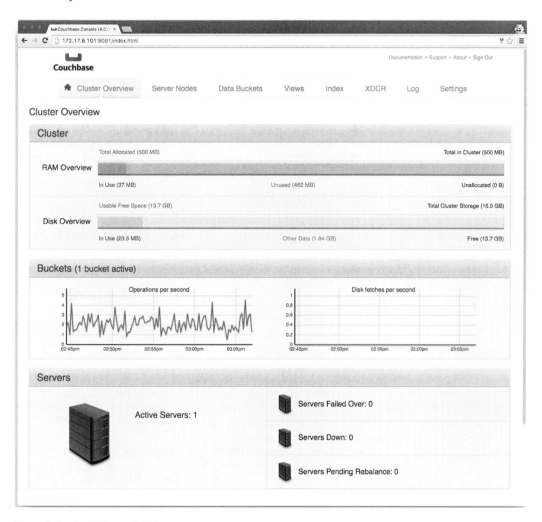

Figure 6.5   Couchbase with data

Listing 6.5   code/ch6/worker/worker.service

```
[Unit]
Description=Worker Service
Requires=flanneld.service
After=flanneld.service

[Service]
TimeoutStartSec=0
RestartSec=10
Restart=always
ExecStartPre=-/usr/bin/docker rm -f worker
ExecStartPre=/usr/bin/docker pull mattbailey/ch6-worker:latest
ExecStart=/usr/bin/docker run --rm --name worker
    -e NODE_ENV=production mattbailey/ch6-worker:latest
ExecStop=-/usr/bin/docker rm -f worker
```

The worker will always exit if it can't find a Couchbase server. Here you give it a little time between startups.

This will remain available on your public Docker Hub account if you want to use it instead of building the app yourself. You use :latest here so you're automatically always using the latest published version.

Passes an env var NODE_ENV=production. This is a general convention for Node.js apps, but you'll use it to configure the app depending on the environment.

The Dockerfile for the worker is also simple and is almost the same as the `helloworld` example, except you don't even have to expose a port.

Listing 6.6   code/ch6/worker/Dockerfile

```
FROM library/node:onbuild
```

Also, create the package.json file for the worker, with a few dependencies.

Listing 6.7   code/ch6/worker/package.json

```
{
  "name": "ch6-worker",
  "version": "1.0.0",
  "description": "Example Worker Process",
  "main": "worker.js",
  "scripts": { "start" : "node worker.js" },
  "dependencies": {
    "couchbase": "^2.1.6",
    "node-etcd": "^4.2.1",
    "websocket": "^1.0.23"
  },
  "author": "m@mdb.io",
  "license": "ISC"
}
```

Tells the node:onbuild Docker container to run this as its entry point

Library for communicating with Couchbase
Library for communicating with etcd
Library for general WebSocket use

That's similar to the `helloworld` app as well, but with the new dependencies. Now, let's look at the worker.

Listing 6.8 code/ch6/worker/worker.js

```
const Etcd = require('node-etcd')
const W3CWebSocket = require('websocket').w3cwebsocket
const couchbase = require('couchbase')
const os = require('os')

const isProd = (process.env.NODE_ENV === 'production')

const thisIp = (isProd) ?
  os.networkInterfaces().eth0
  .filter(v => v.family === 'IPv4')[0].address
  : '127.0.0.1'
const etcdAddress = (isProd) ?
  thisIp
  .split('.').slice(0,3).concat(['1'])
  .join('.') : '127.0.0.1'

const etcd = new Etcd(etcdAddress, '2379')
const couchbaseWatcher = etcd
  .watcher('services/couchbase', null, {recursive: true})

couchbaseWatcher.on('set', newCouchbase => {
  console.log('new couchbase config',
    newCouchbase.body.node.nodes)
  process.exit(0)
})

const connection = (process.env.NODE_ENV === 'production') ?
  `couchbase://${etcd.getSync('services/couchbase', {recursive: true})
    .body.node.nodes.map(v => v.value).join(',')}` :
  'couchbase://127.0.0.1'

  console.log('current connection:', connection)
  const client = new W3CWebSocket('ws://stream.meetup.com/2/rsvps')
  const cluster = new couchbase.Cluster(connection)
  const bucket = cluster.openBucket('default')
  function store(data) {
    bucket.upsert(Date.now().toString(),data || 'empty',() => {})
  }
  client.onmessage = data => { store(JSON.parse(data.data).event) }
```

Gets the IP address for eth0 in the container (the flannel address) if you're in production; localhost otherwise

If you're in production, figures out the IP on which you can access etcd

Creates an event emitter for watching this etcd endpoint (the one the Couchbase sidekick sets)

Logging, so you can see in the journal that the worker is going to restart, and why

If you're not in production, sets the connection string to localhost (for development)

Assembles a connection-string URI for the Couchbase connection from the contents of keys under services/couchbase/

If the watcher sees a set event on any Couchbase etcd key, it will exit the worker, causing systemd to restart it.

Pushes the data into Couchbase when the client emits a message

Database insert function, using a datestamp as the key

WebSocket client connection to the Meetup.com RSVP stream

Logging, so you can see how the worker is trying to connect

If this looks a little daunting, or you have little or no JavaScript experience, that's okay; we'll go through the code step by step. There's a lot here that isn't important for this book: to remove that from your cognitive load, the `require()` statements at the top import libraries, and many of the unannotated lines at the end get set up to write to the Couchbase server. I've used a lot of shorthand for the sake of page length, but this is what you should take away as the program's step-by-step process:

1   Determines its own IP address in flannel (only so you can figure out the etcd IP); for example, 10.1.1.3
2   Figures out the etcd IP; for example, 10.1.1.1
3   Sets up a watch on the etcd keys for Couchbase
4   Exits the program if there are any *new* keys in /services/couchbase/
5   Puts together a connection string from etcd keys in /services/couchbase/ (for example, `couchbase://10.1.1.2`)
6   Listens to the RSVP socket, and writes its messages to Couchbase

You'll notice that *most* of this program deals with the context of the CoreOS environment. The functional worker part is only the last five lines. Of course, this is a simple example; but you can see how sometimes, putting this kind of contextual logic outside of a unit file can make it a little easier to do complex logic for services based on the cluster state.

Now, you can get your worker service running! But *be warned*: you're connecting a *live* service that will immediately start writing a stream to your database. This stream is pretty slow—maybe four events per second—but if you forget to stop the worker, you'll fill up your VM's hard drive. Also, be sure you're going to run only one worker. Fleet should prevent you from running multiple workers, but if you manage to do so, Meetup.com will probably eventually blacklist your IP address for an unknown amount of time. With that in mind, fire it up and begin looking at your log:

```
$ fleetctl start code/ch6/worker/worker.service
Unit worker.service launched on 72476ea6.../172.17.8.101
$ fleetctl journal -f worker
...
May 27 21:44:30 core-01 systemd[1]: Started Worker Service.      ⊲── You should see a successful start ...
...
May 27 21:44:31 core-01 docker[14982]: current connection: couchbase://10.1.1.2
```

... and a Couchbase URI that makes sense.

If you opened the web admin port for Couchbase when you started it, you can now go visit it (http://172.17.8.101:8091/) and see data coming in. It should look something like figure 6.5 at the beginning of this section: the main admin page should show one bucket active, with a nice graph showing activity in operations per second.

Congratulations! You now have a full data-aggregation system! This is the kind of pattern you can follow for any worker-type program that you want to deploy on

CoreOS. Things like aggregators, crawlers, and scientific computing workers all fit well in this model. Next, let's move on to the web app, so you can look at some of the data.

6.3.2 *The web application*

Much like the worker, you're going to do most of the complex context configuration in the application logic, so the service unit is equally simple. The only difference is that you'll run multiple instances, so you need to make a template, shown in the next listing. This is a simple app that just displays some data to prove that everything you've set up is working properly; at the end of this chapter, you'll have a site that looks something like figure 6.6.

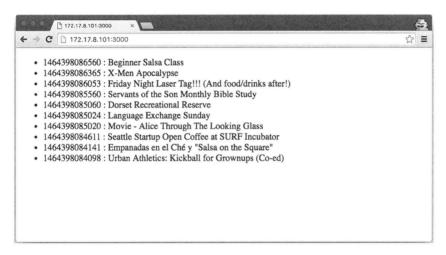

Figure 6.6   Exciting killer app

Listing 6.9   code/ch6/webapp/web@.service

```
[Unit]
Description=Express and Socket.io Web Service %i
Requires=flanneld.service
After=flanneld.service

[Service]
TimeoutStartSec=0
RestartSec=5
Restart=always
ExecStartPre=-/usr/bin/docker rm -f web-%i
ExecStartPre=/usr/bin/docker pull mattbailey/ch6-web:latest
ExecStart=/usr/bin/docker run \
  --rm \
  -p 3000:3000 \                       One small difference from the
  -e NODE_ENV=production \             worker is that you expose a port.
  --name web-%i \
  mattbailey/ch6-web:latest
```

```
ExecStop=-/usr/bin/docker rm -f web-%i
```

```
[X-Fleet]
Conflicts=web@*.service          ◁──────┐  Because you expose a port, more than
                                         └  one can't run on the same machine.
```

Like the mattbailey/ch6-worker image, I'll leave this on the Docker Hub in case you
don't want to build it from the Dockerfile yourself—which brings us to the simple
Dockerfile (it's the same as the one from the `helloworld` examples).

Listing 6.10   code/ch6/webapp/Dockerfile

```
FROM library/node:onbuild
EXPOSE 3000
```

The package.json file is also similar.

Listing 6.11   code/ch6/webapp/package.json

```json
{
  "name": "ch6-web",
  "version": "1.0.0",
  "description": "Example Web App",
  "main": "app.js",
  "scripts": { "start" : "node app.js" },
  "dependencies": {
    "connect-memcached": "^0.2.0",
    "couchbase": "^2.1.6",
    "express": "^4.13.4",
    "express-session": "^1.13.0",
    "node-etcd": "^4.2.1",
    "socket.io": "^1.4.6"
  },
  "author": "m@mdb.io",
  "license": "ISC"
}
```

This pulls in a few more libraries for Express, memcached, and Socket.IO. Before we
get into the back-end application, let's look at the single index.html file you'll serve a
user (see listing 6.11). This is essentially a single-page application, meaning the server
isn't serving up any HTML in a dynamic way: it's serving up a single document, and the
rest of the elements are dynamically created by JavaScript (well, JSX, to be specific)
within the page. This JavaScript only runs in the browser, and it also watches the
`socket.io` WebSocket for messages so it can update the page without requiring any
navigation. I'm using a UI framework called React for this, mostly because it's currently
popular and, again, terse enough that it doesn't take up too much room in the text.

Listing 6.12 code/ch6/webapp/index.html

This and the three scripts below it are libraries that give you the ability to write JSX within the page.

socket.io will serve up this script from the web app to set up the WebSocket connection.

This and the CSS file below it are a simple YouTube-style progress bar called NProgress to give you an indication that things are working when you view the site.

```html
<!DOCTYPE html>
<html>
  <head>
    <script src="https://cdnjs.cloudflare.com/ajax/libs
    /react/15.1.0/react.min.js"></script>
    <script src="https://cdnjs.cloudflare.com/ajax/libs
    react/15.1.0/react-dom.min.js"></script>
    <script src="https://cdnjs.cloudflare.com/ajax/libs
    /babel-core/5.8.23/browser.min.js"></script>
    <script src="https://cdnjs.cloudflare.com/ajax/libs
    /nprogress/0.2.0/nprogress.min.js"></script>
    <link rel="stylesheet" href="https://cdnjs.cloudflare.com/ajax/libs
    /nprogress/0.2.0/nprogress.min.css">
    <script src="/socket.io/socket.io.js"></script>
  </head>
  <body>
    <div id="mount-point"></div>
    <script type="text/babel">
    const Rsvps = React.createClass({
      _onMessage: function(data) {this.setState({items: data})},
      getInitialState: function() { return { items: [] } },
      render: function() {
        const createItem = (item) =>
          { return <li>{ item.key } : { item.value }</li> }
        return <ul>{ this.state.items.map(createItem) }</ul>
      }
    })
    const rsvps = ReactDOM
      .render(<Rsvps />, document.getElementById('mount-point'))
    const meetupSocket = io()
    meetupSocket.on('message', (data) => {
      NProgress.start()
      rsvps._onMessage(data)
      NProgress.done()
    })
    </script>
  </body>
</html>
```

In this listener, if a message is seen on meetupSocket, you update the element with the _onMessage function in the Rsvps class.

Every React component has a render method that creates the page elements.

Updates the state of the component (with new data)

Creates the dynamic unordered list <ul> element to display the RSVPs

Sets up the socket.io event emitter

Mounts the Rsvps element to the <div id="mount-point"></div> element

If you don't have much experience with client-side JavaScript programming, don't worry; most of this serves to build a dynamic element. Fundamentally, this code is similar to the code in the worker! It listens to a WebSocket and updates the page when it gets a new message, the same way the worker listens to a WebSocket and updates Couchbase. Ultimately, this is just a view, and it's not important for you to know about it in depth for this example; but it's the simplest way to show that your web app is working, and it will absolutely be part of any complete web application.

How do you serve this HTML and JavaScript? With more JavaScript, of course! The following listing shows the application server.

Listing 6.13   code/ch6/webapp/app.js

```
const Etcd = require('node-etcd')
const path = require('path')
const app = require('express')()
const http = require('http').Server(app)
const session = require('express-session')
const MemcacheStore = require('connect-memcached')(session)
const couchbase = require('couchbase')
const io = require('socket.io')(http)
const os = require('os')

const isProd = (process.env.NODE_ENV === 'production')

const thisIp = (isProd) ?
  os.networkInterfaces().eth0
  .filter(v => v.family === 'IPv4')[0].address
  : '127.0.0.1'
const etcdAddress = (isProd) ?
  thisIp
  .split('.').slice(0,3).concat(['1'])
  .join('.') : '127.0.0.1'

const etcd = new Etcd(etcdAddress, '2379')
const memcacheWatcher = etcd
  .watcher('services/memcached', null, {recursive: true})
const couchbaseWatcher = etcd
  .watcher('services/couchbase', null, {recursive: true})

couchbaseWatcher.on('set', newCouchbase => {
  console.log('new couchbase config', newCouchbase)
  process.exit(0)
})
memcacheWatcher.on('set', newMemcache => {
  console.log('new memcache config', newMemcache)
  process.exit(0)
})

const config = (isProd) ?
{
  couchbase: `couchbase://${etcd.getSync('services/couchbase',
  {recursive: true})
    .body.node.nodes.map(v => v.value).join(',')}`,
  memcached: etcd.getSync('services/memcached', {recursive: true})
```

> **Event emitter for changes to etcd keys in services/memcached**

> **Uses an object instead of a string to set configuration, so you can get the config for Couchbase and memcached at the same time**

**Initializes the memcached
session store**

**To read data from Couchbase, you have to assemble a
map function as a view. This is a simple one that emits
the RSVP ID and Meetup event name.**

> **Similar to the Couchbase
config, returns an array or
your memcached instances**

**Housekeeping in Couchbase that gives
the app the ability to create views**

```
      .body.node.nodes.map(v => `${v.value}:11211`)
} : {
  couchbase: 'couchbase://127.0.0.1',
  memcached: ['127.0.0.1:11211']
}

console.log('current config:', config)

const cluster = new couchbase.Cluster(config.couchbase)
const memStore = new MemcacheStore({ hosts: config.memcached })

const bucket = cluster.openBucket('default')
const bucketMgr = bucket.manager()
const ddocdata = {views:{by_id:{ map:'function (doc) {
  emit(doc.event_id, doc.event_name) }'}}}
bucketMgr.upsertDesignDocument('ddocid', ddocdata, () => {})
const query = couchbase.ViewQuery
  .from('ddocid', 'by_id').order(2).limit(10)
app.use(session({
  saveUninitialized:true,
  resave: false,store: memStore,
  secret: 'coreosinaction' }))
app.get('/', (req, res) =>
  res.sendFile('./index.html', {root: path.join(__dirname)}))
io.on('connection', socket =>
  setInterval(() =>
    bucket.query(query, (err, results) =>
      io.emit('message', results)), 5000))

http.listen(3000)
```

**Saves the view
to the bucket**

**Query that uses the
view, limiting it to
returning 10 results
in reverse-key order**

**Sets up express-
session to use the
memcached store
as its back end**

**Sets up socket.io to run, and
emits the results of the query
(bucket.query()) every 5
seconds (5000 ms) to any
connected client**

**Serves up the index.html
file at the / URL**

**Opens the HTTP listener
for clients to connect**

This looks like a lot to take in, especially if you're unfamiliar with Node.js. If you didn't read the section about the worker (section 6.3.1), be sure go to back, because a lot of things are duplicated here.

Libraries are imported at the top, and then you have a lot of the same contextual logic as in the worker, to generate a connection to memcached and Couchbase and exit the program if they change. The only difference here is that you do it for both memcached and Couchbase; you only had Couchbase to worry about in the worker.

Once you get down into the (again, relatively small, compared to the context code) application logic, a few more things are going on:

1   You set up a view in Couchbase. It's not important how this functions, just that you need one to query data from Couchbase. You can think of it as a stored procedure, if you're used to SQL.

2   You set up a session that sets a cookie in the browser. It's backed by your memcached cluster but not used for anything.

3   You serve up the single index.html file at /.

4   For every connection to the WebSocket, you begin sending queried data back to the client every 5 seconds.

5   For clarity, *both* the WebSocket and HTTP data are served over port 3000.

That's it! Now you can deploy the client-facing web service. Start up three web units with fleet, and (optionally) watch the journal output:

```
$ fleetctl start code/ch6/webapp/web@{1..3}.service
...
$ fleetctl journal -f web@1
...
May 27 23:29:12 core-02 systemd[1]:
 ➥Started Express and Socket.io Web Service 1.
...
May 27 23:29:13 core-02 docker[10696]:
 ➥current config: { couchbase: 'couchbase://10.1.1.2',
May 27 23:29:13 core-02 docker[10696]:
 ➥memcached: [ '10.1.35.2:11211', '10.1.57.2:11211', '10.1.35.3:11211' ] }
```

The web application started up successfully. Let's look at all the services running now.

Listing 6.14   All units

```
UNIT                        MACHINE                    ACTIVE    SUB
couchbase-sidekick@1.service    72476ea6.../172.17.8.101    active    running
couchbase@1.service             72476ea6.../172.17.8.101    active    running
memcached-sidekick@1.service    ac6b3188.../172.17.8.103    active    running
memcached-sidekick@2.service    b598f557.../172.17.8.102    active    running
memcached-sidekick@3.service    ac6b3188.../172.17.8.103    active    running
memcached@1.service             ac6b3188.../172.17.8.103    active    running
memcached@2.service             b598f557.../172.17.8.102    active    running
memcached@3.service             ac6b3188.../172.17.8.103    active    running
web@1.service                   72476ea6.../172.17.8.101    active    running
web@2.service                   b598f557.../172.17.8.102    active    running
web@3.service                   ac6b3188.../172.17.8.103    active    running
worker.service                  72476ea6.../172.17.8.101    active    running
```

You should be able to visit any of those hosts on port 3000 (for example, http://172.17.8.103:3000) and see your fantastic new web app! The page should update itself every 5 seconds from the socket.io event and show new data. You've successfully deployed your first custom, full-stack application to a CoreOS cluster, but there's still more work to do.

6.4 *Where to from here?*

Now that you've built out your application stack on CoreOS, how do you test for failure, and what does the next iteration look like? This section works through both of these items and leads into the next chapter. By the end of this section, you should be able to test the resilience of your application and have an idea of how to improve what you've started. I talk a lot about fault tolerance in this book, so let's begin with an outage.

6.4.1 *Responding to failure*

As with any complex deployed application, you want to be able to test failures in your systems. With the caveat that data loss in the Couchbase database will happen (in this chapter) if the machine the Couchbase server is running on goes down, your entire application stack should survive the failure of one machine pretty gracefully. Remember, though, that in a three-machine cluster, etcd can't re-achieve quorum with a single node. In a real-world deployment, you'd always provision enough machines because you'd expect cluster partitioning to occur, as previously discussed in section 4.3.

To see what's going on, you'll need to open two terminals: one to run the commands to break a machine, and one to follow the log of a machine you're not breaking to see how the services respond. The maximum failure would be to kill the node that Couchbase is running on. You know that will cause data loss, but the service should still migrate to another machine in the cluster.

In one terminal, check to find a machine that Couchbase *isn't* running on, and follow the journal of the web service running on that machine:

```
$ fleetctl list-units | grep -E 'web|couchbase@'
couchbase@1.service    7c5009d9.../172.17.8.102   active   running
web@1.service       a54ea5bc.../172.17.8.103   active   running
web@2.service       7c5009d9.../172.17.8.102   active   running
web@3.service       9e08f1b2.../172.17.8.101   active   running
$ fleetctl journal -lines 2 -f web@1
-- Logs begin at Sat 2016-05-28 04:13:47 UTC. --
May 28 04:29:46 core-03 docker[2964]:
 current config: { couchbase: 'couchbase://10.1.15.2',
May 28 04:29:46 core-03 docker[2964]:
 memcached: [ '10.1.58.3:11211', '10.1.58.2:11211', '10.1.53.2:11211' ] }
```

> Looks like web@1 is running on a machine that couchbase@1 isn't, so let's follow its log.

Now, you're following the log for web@1. You can see the output of its log from the initial configuration, connecting to your three memcached instances and Couchbase. In a new terminal, kill core-02, where Couchbase and one memcached instance are running (first, make sure you're in the directory where your Vagrantfile is located):

```
$ vagrant halt core-02
==> core-02: Attempting graceful shutdown of VM...
```

> ### halt vs. destroy
>
> Note that you always use `vagrant halt` in these scenarios rather than the more forceful `vagrant destroy`. The behavior would be the same for the cluster when it goes down (you can try it yourself if you want: it's more like pulling the power cord).
>
> What's different with `vagrant destroy` is that you can't have that node rejoin the cluster with `vagrant up`—not because it isn't possible in CoreOS, but because the Vagrant scripts do a number of bootstrapping things to brand-new nodes that they don't do to a node that's just stopped, so you end up with a node all by itself. In the real world, you wouldn't do the bootstrapping things that Vagrant does, so you can remove and add nodes at will.

Let's look back at the terminal where you were following the journal of web@1:

```
May 28 04:40:38 core-03 docker[2964]: new couchbase config{ action: 'set',
May 28 04:40:38 core-03 docker[2964]:   node:
May 28 04:40:38 core-03 docker[2964]:    { key: '/services/couchbase/1',
May 28 04:40:38 core-03 docker[2964]:      value: '10.1.53.5',
...
May 28 04:40:43 core-03 systemd[1]:
web@1.service: Service hold-off time over, scheduling restart.
May 28 04:40:43 core-03 systemd[1]:
Stopped Express and Socket.io Web Service 1.
...
May 28 04:40:45 core-03 systemd[1]:
Started Express and Socket.io Web Service 1.
...
May 28 04:40:46 core-03 docker[7141]:
current config: { couchbase: 'couchbase://10.1.53.5',
May 28 04:40:46 core-03 docker[7141]:
memcached: [ '10.1.58.3:11211', '10.1.58.2:11211', '10.1.53.2:11211' ] }
```

Log from the etcd.watch() emitter

Log from the app after it starts up again and generates a new configuration

6.4.2   *What's missing?*

A few things are missing from this example. First is the reliability of the data store, which we'll address in the next chapter.

Second, you now have three servers running your edge service (the web app). At some point, you'll need to put a load balancer in front of them, and that may mean adding some new sidekicks to your web services or extending the application to provide a health-check endpoint. How that's implemented is up to you. Optionally, you could also do some clever round-robin DNS setup; for example, AWS Route 53 has health checks built in that can change the DNS, as long as you're comfortable with a downtime the length of the DNS TTL for some clients if one goes down.

Finally, there are a lot of magic numbers in the application configuration of ports, timeouts, and so on. Optimally, in a production environment, you'll want to abstract all these into etcd and use it as your central source of truth, so you can configure these items when you need to.

6.5 *Summary*

- Have a plan of attack in applying complex architectures to CoreOS.
- Figure out how to test each part of your stack in isolation.
- Determine which parts of your stack need to be redundant.
- Understand the order of events when parts fail.
- Try to identify the shortcomings of your implementations (in this case, data loss if the Couchbase machine fails).

Big Data stack 7

This chapter covers

- Adding reliability to the data store from chapter 6
- Managing a distributed persistent data store in CoreOS
- Simulating failures in the data system

In this chapter, you'll build a Big Data aggregation platform that seeds a database with random search queries against Twitter. You'll build a small corpus of data, make Twitter rate-limit you (while still being a good API citizen), and see how to take care of your mission-critical (although random) data. Your application will function like this:

1 Six stateless workers will generate a random word and search for it on the Twitter API.
2 The results will be stored in Couchbase.
3 Workers will continue to search every 100 ms in parallel until they're rate limited.
4 Once they're rate limited, they'll set a distributed lock in etcd with a 15-minute TTL.
5 All workers will fast-exit on the presence of that lock.
6 When the lock expires, workers will start over at step 1.

This will be an evolution of the application from chapter 6, so you must finish that project first. You're moving to a distributed data system that will give you more performance, greater capacity, and higher availability. You're also moving to a data source that will allow you to have multiple simultaneous connections to it, unlike the Meetup.com stream. This lets you play with a swarm of workers and control them with a distributed lock.

7.1 Scope of this chapter's example

This expansion on the example from chapter 6 will make Couchbase a part of your system that is resilient to failure and that provides some simple vectors for high availability and scaling for performance. Couchbase is certainly an overkill tool for the previous example; but this chapter goes through what it takes to use a system like Couchbase as a Big Data platform in CoreOS, which is what Couchbase is intended for. Of course, you won't be adding petabytes of data to your local Couchbase cluster, but this example will show you what that kind of architecture can look like in CoreOS.

We'll also take another look at the worker and some models of how to use etcd in CoreOS as a distributed lock scheduler for large-scale data acquisition. And, of course, we'll finish with fault-testing scenarios that use this new persistent store and contain mission-critical data.

To achieve some of these goals with Couchbase, you'll have to write additional custom software (Node.js) to orchestrate the automatic management of the cluster. This piece of orchestration software is by far the largest program in this book; and because there's no expectation that you know JavaScript, I'll break it down into a few parts and explain them one by one.

7.1.1 Adding to the architecture

Figure 7.1 shows how the architecture will look once you're finished with this chapter. As you can see, it includes a few new components. The workers have expanded to a small army of programs to more efficiently gather data from various sources, and the Couchbase persistent store is now a cluster of units that will share and balance data.

You'll be deploying as many Couchbase units as you have CoreOS machines. Much like etcd, Couchbase has limitations for failure states. In a cluster of three nodes, you can retain only one extra copy of replicated data in a Couchbase cluster. The same formula applies (as discussed in chapter 3): $floor((N-1)/2)$, where N is the number of nodes. This represents the *maximum* number of replicas you can set, but you *can* set fewer than the maximum. For example, with seven nodes, you could have three replicas and therefore lose three nodes at the same time and have no data loss; but you could also have just one replica with seven nodes, if you chose. You don't have a choice with three nodes, though: you get one replica and one failure.

Before you get started, give yourself a clean slate using `vagrant destroy -f &&` `vagrant up`. Now let's look at your data source.

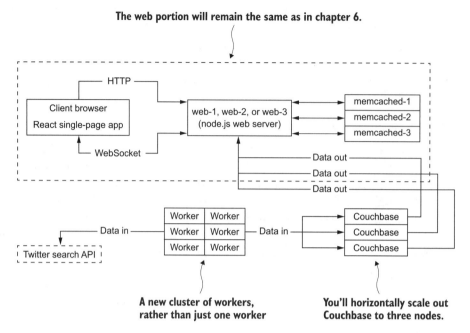

Figure 7.1   Big Data architecture

7.1.2   *New data source*

The new data source for this project is Twitter. If you're so inclined, you're welcome to change the code to fetch from any API. Like pretty much all public APIs these days, Twitter requires that you generate a Twitter API key for you to connect with. Its primary purpose is to rate-limit you if you hit the API too much. This is perfect for this example, because you'll hit the rate limit intentionally to see how to use a distributed lock in etcd to throttle your workers. It'll also give you the opportunity to set some extra configuration in etcd. So, begin by making a Twitter account if you don't have one, and then follow these steps:

1 At https://twitter.com/settings/devices, enter your mobile number (this is required in order to create a key).
2 Go to https://apps.twitter.com/, and click Create New App.
3 Enter whatever you want in the three required fields. You can leave Callback URL blank. Click Create Your Twitter Application.
4 Once you're in the application settings, click the Keys and Access Token tab.
5 You can optionally change Access Level to read-only, because you'll only be reading data.
6 At the bottom, click Create My Access Token.

7 Save the following information somewhere handy:
  - Consumer Key (API Key)
  - Consumer Secret (API Secret)
  - Access Token
  - Access Token Secret

With all that information gathered, open a session to your CoreOS cluster, and store it to etcd:

```
$ etcdctl set /config/worker/auth '{ "consumer_key":"Your Consumer Key",
➥"consumer_secret":"Your Consumer Secret", "access_token_key":
➥"Your Access Token",
➥"access_token_secret":"Your Access Token Secret" }'   ⟵┐ Set your values for
                                                         │ each of these items.
```

Now that you've got some initial configuration in place, let's dive into the new components. We'll start with the worker, because the changes there are minimal, and then move on to the brand-new program to orchestrate your storage.

7.2 New stack components

You won't change your web application at all in this chapter. For simplicity, you'll adjust the worker to store the data in Couchbase with the same schema so you don't have to touch the Express app. But you'll make some significant changes to how you manage the database, which is why an entire chapter is dedicated to managing this distributed persistence. If you skipped over anything in chapter 6, you should go back and run through the full example, or the code in this chapter won't make much sense.

7.2.1 Twitter scraper

You do have to make some changes to the worker, both for the new data source and so that you can run as many workers as you want. Nothing is different in the worker Dockerfile (it's still just one line), but make the following changes in the package.json file.

Listing 7.1 code/ch7/worker/package.json

```
{
  "name": "ch7-worker",          ⟵─── Simple name change
  "version": "1.0.0",
  "description": "Example Worker Process",
  "main": "worker.js",
  "scripts": { "start": "node worker.js" },
  "dependencies": {
    "couchbase": "^2.1.6",
    "node-etcd": "^4.2.1",                      Library that generates a
    "random-word": "^1.0.2",   ⟵───────────┘   random English word
    "twitter": "^1.3.0"        ⟵───┐ The twitter library
  },                               │ simplifies API access.
  "author": "m@mdb.io",
  "license": "ISC"
}
```

You've also removed the websocket library, because you no longer need it. Next, let's look at the new unit template.

Listing 7.2   code/ch7/worker/worker@.service

```
[Unit]
Description=Worker Service %i
Requires=flanneld.service
After=flanneld.service

[Service]
TimeoutStartSec=0
RestartSec=10
Restart=always
ExecStartPre=-/usr/bin/docker rm -f worker-%i
ExecStartPre=/usr/bin/docker pull mattbailey/ch7-worker:latest
ExecStart=/usr/bin/docker run --rm --name worker-%i -e \
    NODE_ENV=production mattbailey/ch7-worker:latest
ExecStop=-/usr/bin/docker rm -f worker-%i
```

> Change the container name, with %i.

> This is where I've posted this worker, if you don't want to build it yourself.

> Change the container name and the image.

> Change the container name again.

This isn't much different than in chapter 6—you're just making it a template and changing the image. Now for the worker, which also looks familiar.

Listing 7.3   code/ch7/worker/worker.js

```
const Etcd = require('node-etcd')
const couchbase = require('couchbase')
const os = require('os')
const Twitter = require('twitter')
const randomWord = require('random-word')

const thisIp = (process.env.NODE_ENV === 'production') ?
  os.networkInterfaces().eth0
  .filter(v => v.family === 'IPv4')[0].address : '127.0.0.1'
const etcdAddress = (process.env.NODE_ENV === 'production') ?
  thisIp .split('.').slice(0,3).concat(['1']).join('.') : '127.0.0.1'

const etcd = new Etcd(etcdAddress, '2379')
const couchbaseWatcher = etcd
  .watcher('services/couchbase', null, {recursive: true})

if (!etcd.getSync('config/worker/lock').err) {
  console.log('lock engaged, exiting')
  process.exit(0)
}

couchbaseWatcher.on('set', newCouchbase => {
  console.log('new couchbase config', newCouchbase.body.node.nodes)
  process.exit(0)
})

const connection = (process.env.NODE_ENV === 'production') ?
  `couchbase://${etcd.getSync('services/couchbase', {recursive: true})
    .body.node.nodes.map(v => v.value).join(',')}` :
  'couchbase://127.0.0.1'
```

> Adds the twitter library as a requirement, and removes the WebSocket client library

> Lets the program exit quickly if it sees a lock set in etcd

```
console.log('current connection:', connection)
const cluster = new couchbase.Cluster(connection)
const bucket = cluster.openBucket('default')
const client = new Twitter(JSON.parse(
  etcd.getSync('config/worker/auth').body.node.value))
function store(data) {bucket.upsert(data.id_str,
  {event_name: data.text}, () => {})}

setInterval(() => {
  const word = randomWord()
  client.get('search/tweets', {q: word}, (err, tweets) => {
    if (err) {
      console.error('Twitter threw error:', err)
      etcd.setSync('config/worker/lock', {ttl: 900})
      process.exit(1)
    }
    console.log(word, tweets.statuses.length)
    if (tweets.statuses.length > 0) {
      tweets.statuses.forEach(tweet => store(tweet))
    }
  })
}, 100)
```

Changes the client to Twitter, using the credentials you set in etcd earlier in the chapter

Slight change here: you'll use the tweet ID as the key and the tweet text as the document content.

Generates a random English word

Queries Twitter for tweets containing that word

If you get an error back from Twitter, it's almost certainly a rate-limit error. This sets a lock on etcd for 15 minutes, which is Twitter's rate-limiting timeout.

If you get back search results (always limited to 15), store them with the store function.

Runs this loop every 100 ms

The program is a little more complex now, but the vast majority of it is the same as in chapter 6. It checks early for a distributed lock; and if Twitter ever throws an error, the program sets a new lock and exits. You only store the tweet text, because tweet metadata is larger than you may think, and you don't want to fill your hard drive. You set the event_name key in the data; this is a holdover from the RSVP schema in chapter 6, and you keep it here so you don't have to change the web application code to view it. You also make sure you only run this query every 100 ms. If you set this number much lower, you're pretty likely to be rate limited in under a second (180 queries), so you artificially throttle the program so you can see what's going on.

You won't start your workers right away, because (especially if you wiped your cluster), you don't have a database yet. Let's move on to the assembly and management of the database.

7.2.2 Orchestrating Couchbase

As I've mentioned many times, maintaining complex, persistent data systems in a fault-tolerant, scalable way is difficult to achieve. There are always a number of edge cases and a lot of things various components have to react to in order for everything to work properly. This is often called *service orchestration*, so I've named the program that does all this for Couchbase *conductor*. This is another reason I like using Node.js: as an event-driven language, it's relatively easy to construct logic on events that can happen in any order, and it's fairly simple for me to show you what's going on.

All that being said, this can seem like a complex application, so I'll break it down into progressive chunks in the conductor.js program. By the end of this section, your Couchbase dashboard should look like figure 7.2.

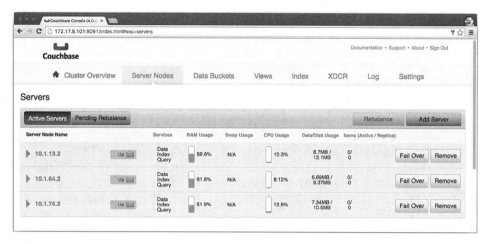

Figure 7.2   Three Couchbase nodes

THE SIMPLE PARTS

First, before we dive into the complexity of conductor, let's go over the things that will look familiar. We'll start with the service unit(s), which have *less* code in them now because you're doing way more logic in the conductor program.

Listing 7.4   code/ch7/couchbase@.service

```
[Unit]
Description=Couchbase Service %i
Requires=flanneld.service
After=flanneld.service

[Service]
TimeoutSec=0
Restart=always
RestartSec=10
ExecStartPre=-/usr/bin/docker kill couchbase-%i
ExecStartPre=-/usr/bin/docker rm -f couchbase-%i
ExecStartPre=/usr/bin/docker pull couchbase:community-4.0.0
ExecStart=/usr/bin/docker run \
  --rm \
  -p 8091:8091 \
  --name couchbase-%i \
  --ulimit nofile=40960:40960 \
  couchbase:community-4.0.0
ExecStop=/usr/bin/docker kill --signal=SIGTERM couchbase-%i

[X-Fleet]
Conflicts=couchbase@*
```

> You add a conflicts line, because you'll be running more than one.

Notice that you removed the ExecStartPost= entry. This will now start up Couchbase and do *no* boostrapping. The couchbase-sidekick@.service will remain *unchanged* for this project. You can copy the one you've already written.

In conductor, I had to add a bit of a strange dependency: there's no API SDK for Couchbase that lets you do administrative actions (such as manipulating the members of a cluster), so I pulled in the official `couchbase-cli` app (which is written in Python) so the program can use it to manipulate the cluster. Annoyingly, Couchbase doesn't distribute this tool independently of the server: you'll have to extract it from the .deb file so that you can pack it in your Docker container. I'll describe how to do that next; or, if you prefer, you can use the container I've put on Docker Hub (mattbailey/ch7-conductor). If you're running on OS X, you'll also have to install `dpkg` via Homebrew in order to extract the tool.

First, download the package from http://mng.bz/8Clk. Then, do the following:

Change the directory to wherever you're storing this program to build your Docker image.

This single command (split over two lines) will extract the correct components.

```
$ cd conductor
$ dpkg --fsys-tarfile \
    ~/Downloads/couchbase-server-community_4.0.0-debian7_amd64.deb | \
tar xf - ./opt/couchbase/bin/couchbase-cli ./opt/couchbase/lib/python
$ ls opt
couchbase
```

You should see a new opt/couchbase directory.

Once you've got that extracted, the following listing shows the simple service unit for conductor.

Listing 7.5   code/ch7/conductor/conductor.service

```
[Unit]
Description=Conductor Service
Requires=flanneld.service
After=flanneld.service

[Service]
TimeoutStartSec=0
RestartSec=5
Restart=always
ExecStartPre=-/usr/bin/docker rm -f conductor
ExecStartPre=/usr/bin/docker pull mattbailey/ch7-conductor:latest
ExecStart=/usr/bin/docker run --rm --name conductor \
    -e NODE_ENV=production mattbailey/ch7-conductor:latest
ExecStop=-/usr/bin/docker rm -f conductor
```

All of that should look familiar—almost identical to the worker. The Dockerfile is also identical to the worker and consists of just one line: `FROM library/node:onbuild`.

Next is package.json, the last item before you dive into the program.

Listing 7.6   code/ch7/conductor/package.json

```
{
  "name": "ch7-conductor",
  "version": "1.0.0",
  "description": "Example Conductor Admin Service",
  "main": "conductor.js",
```

```
    "scripts": { "start" : "node conductor.js" },
    "dependencies": {
      "node-etcd": "^4.2.1"
    },
    "author": "m@mdb.io",
    "license": "ISC"
}
```

Nothing much exciting here either: it has only one dependency, the etcd library. Now, let's get into the meat of the logic: the conductor program.

CONDUCTING THE ORCHESTRA

The beginning of the program isn't particularly interesting and looks like many of the other programs you've seen in this book.

Listing 7.7   code/ch7/conductor/conductor.js—section 1

```
const Etcd = require('node-etcd')
const spawn = require('child_process').spawn          ◁———    Lets you spawn
const os = require('os')                                       child processes (for
                                                              couchbase-cli)
const thisIp = (process.env.NODE_ENV === 'production') ?
  os.networkInterfaces().eth0
  .filter(v => v.family === 'IPv4')[0].address : '127.0.0.1'
const etcdAddress = (process.env.NODE_ENV === 'production') ?
  thisIp .split('.').slice(0,3).concat(['1']).join('.') : '127.0.0.1'

const etcd = new Etcd(etcdAddress, '2379')                    Adds one more
const cbWatcher = etcd                                        watcher than usual,
  .watcher('services/couchbase', null, {recursive:true})      to watch the config
const cbConfigWatcher = etcd                                  you'll set for
    .watcher('config/couchbase', null, {recursive:true})  ◁——  Couchbase
```

This listing sets up the etcd connection and watches a few keys, as you've done in all of this book's other applications.

Next, you'll automate the construction of the Couchbase configuration and fall back to a static default.

Listing 7.8   code/ch7/conductor/conductor.js—section 2

Attempts to fetch an existing config from etcd

Default configuration

Sets a flag to let the program know this (initially) isn't a new cluster

Initially sets the config for the program to be empty

```
const cbDefaultConfig = {
   password: 'Password1',
   nodes: 3,
   bucket: 'default',
   ram: 500
}

let cbConfigGet = etcd.getSync('config/couchbase', {recursive:true})
let cbConfig = {}
let newCluster = false
```

If the fetch from etcd returns an error, sets the default config in etcd instead…   **…and sets the program config to the default…**   **…and tells the program this is a new cluster, because there was no prior config**

```
if (cbConfigGet.err) {
  console.log('no config, setting default:', cbDefaultConfig)
  Object.keys(cbDefaultConfig).forEach(key => etcd
    .setSync(`config/couchbase/${key}`, cbDefaultConfig[key]))
  cbConfig = cbDefaultConfig
  newCluster = true
} else {
  cbConfig = cbConfigGet.body.node.nodes.reduce((p, c) => {
    p[c.key.split('/').slice(-1)[0]] = c.value
    return p
  }, {})
}
console.log('LOADED CONFIG:', cbConfig)
```

Logs the output

If fetching the config was successful, maps the values from etcd to the single cbConfig object

This listing sets up some config for the rest of the program with context from etcd if it's there, or a default if it's not. There's a lot of logic here, but there's also room for improvement; you may want to set the default config in etcd as well, but for simplicity in this case, you set it statically.

Let's move on and set up how you'll communicate with the Couchbase nodes.

Listing 7.9   code/ch7/conductor/conductor.js—section 3

Exits if no data was set by sidekicks

Path to the couchbase-cli program you pulled in at the beginning of the section. The Dockerfile placed it here.

Fetches from etcd all the node data your Couchbase sidekicks set

```
const nodeGet = etcd.getSync('services/couchbase', {recursive:true})

if (nodeGet.err || !nodeGet.body.node.nodes) {
  console.log('NO NODES FOUND, EXITING')
  process.exit(1)
}

const CB_CLI = '/usr/src/app/opt/couchbase/bin/couchbase-cli'
const CB_OPTS = ['-u', 'Administrator', '-p', cbConfig.password, '-c']
let FIRST_NODE = nodeGet.body.node.nodes[0].value

const cb = (cmd, ip = '127.0.0.1', flags = [], defaultOpts = CB_OPTS) =>
  spawn(CB_CLI, [cmd, ...defaultOpts, `${ip}:8091`, ...flags])
```

Basic options almost every couchbase-cli command needs

Function that returns a function to call couchbase-cli with all the right flags

You need to get the IP address of any one node here. This picks the first one returned.

If you want to look up the `couchbase-cli` documentation for reference, you can find it at http://mng.bz/I915. Most of this code pretty self-explanatory, except the last line. As I mentioned, because there's no SDK (Node.js or otherwise) to interact with the administrative operations of Couchbase, you're spawning out to `couchbase-cli`; this code essentially generates a function that resembles what an SDK might look like, with some built-in default flags. So, every time you want to call `couchbase-cli`, it's as easy as `cb(<command>, <IP Address>, [<flags>, …])`?

Next, let's go into each of the discrete functions before you call any of them.

Listing 7.10 code/ch7/conductor/conductor.js: `initCluster()`

```
function initCluster(callback) {
  const replicas = nodes => Math.floor((parseInt(nodes)-1)/2)

  if (newCluster) {
    cb('cluster-init', FIRST_NODE, [
      '--cluster-username=Administrator',
      `--cluster-password=${cbConfig.password}`,
      '--services=data,index,query',
      `--cluster-ramsize=${cbConfig.ram}`
    ], ['-c']).stdout.on('data', initOut => {
      console.log('cluster-init:', initOut.toString())
      if (initOut.toString().match(/ERROR/)) { process.exit(1) }
      cb('bucket-create', FIRST_NODE, [
        `--bucket=${cbConfig.bucket}`,
        `--bucket-type=couchbase`,
        `--bucket-ramsize=${cbConfig.ram}`,
        `--bucket-replica=${replicas(cbConfig.nodes)}`,
        `--cluster-ramsize=${cbConfig.ram}`
      ]).stdout.on('data', createOut => {
        callback(`bucket-
      create: ${createOut.toString()}`)
      })
    })
  } else {
    callback('cluster & bucket already initialized')
  }
}
```

Inner function that provides a formula for the maximum number of replicas you can have for as many nodes as you have

When this function is called, does a cluster-init if this is a new cluster

If cluster-init fails, exits immediately because something really bad happened

Creates your initial default bucket

Executes the callback, and returns log data

If this isn't a new cluster, calls the callback

This is the main function you'll call at the end of the program to initialize the cluster of Couchbase nodes. These are the same commands you used in chapter 6's `couchbase@.service` unit to do the same thing: `cluster-init` and `bucket-create` to create your default bucket. There's some room for improvement here, too: you might want to create a bunch of buckets from etcd keys with different parameters, such as number of replicas or RAM size. You're using the formula for the maximum number of replicas for the number of nodes you have here because your data is "super important."

Next is the `addNode()` function.

Listing 7.11 code/ch7/conductor/conductor.js: `addNode()`

```
function addNode(newNode) {
  console.log('attempting to add:', newNode)
  return new Promise(resolve => {
    cb('server-add', FIRST_NODE, [
      `--server-add=${newNode}`,
```

Issues the server-add command to add a node to a cluster

```
          '--server-add-username=Administrator',
          `--server-add-password=${cbConfig.password}`,
          '--services=data,index,query'
      ]).stdout.on('data', addOut => {
        resolve(addOut.toString())
      })
    })
  })
}
```

This function takes an IP address as an argument and adds a Couchbase node to the cluster. There's some new logic you haven't seen before: this function returns a `Promise`, which is a function that gives you more control over asynchronous flow. It's not critical that you know how it works; it just lets you add multiple nodes at once and then do `initialAdd()` (shown in the next listing) once all the `Promises` generated by this function resolve.

> **Listing 7.12 code/ch7/conductor/conductor.js: `initialAdd()`**

```
function initialAdd() {
  if (nodeGet.body.node.nodes.length > 1) {
    const notFirstNode = nodeGet.body.node.nodes.filter(v => v.value !==
    FIRST_NODE)                                              ◁——————  Gets all IPs of
    console.log('found other nodes:', notFirstNode)                   Couchbase nodes that
    Promise.all(notFirstNode.map(node =>                              aren't FIRST_NODE
    addNode(node.value))).then(res => {               ◁——————
      console.log(res)                                                Runs addNode() (from
      setTimeout(rebalanceCluster, 10000)   ◁——————                  listing 7.11) on each of
    })                                                                the IPs at the same time
  }                       Once both nodes are added, waits
}                         10 seconds and runs rebalanceCluster()
                          (see listing 7.13) once.
```

In Couchbase, you want to add all of your nodes and then rebalance your data once (see listing 7.13), or you're going to waste a lot of processing power. As is the case for many NoSQL servers with clustering capabilities, when you add nodes to the cluster, an extra step is usually required to spread the data around to all nodes. This is necessary in order for the replicas to distribute themselves and keep your data safe.

> **Listing 7.13 code/ch7/conductor/conductor.js: `rebalanceCluster()`**

```
function rebalanceCluster() {
  cb('rebalance', FIRST_NODE)
    .stdout.on('data', rebalanceOut => {
      console.log(rebalanceOut.toString())
    })
}
```

All this function does is issue a single rebalance command. It only needs to be run on one node to be cluster-wide.

Next is the `failNode()` function, which you'll use later when you see a node disappear from etcd.

```
function failNode(failedNode, callback) {
  cb('failover', FIRST_NODE, [
    `--server-failover=${failedNode}`
  ]).stdout.on('data', failedOut => {
    callback(failedOut)
  })
}
```

Couchbase has some automatic failover capabilities, but the minimum timeout is 30 seconds for those to kick in. If you see a node disappear from etcd, you'll want to remove it immediately.

The next listing contains all of your event listeners for elements in etcd.

```
cbWatcher.on('set', newCouchbase => {          ◁——— If a new node is added to etcd, then...
  setTimeout(() => {
    addNode(newCouchbase.node.value)           ◁——— ...add the node after seconds, and...
      .then(msg => {
        console.log('Node added, rebalancing:', msg)      ...issue another rebalance
        setTimeout(rebalanceCluster, 5000)      ◁———      after another 5 seconds.
      })
  }, 5000)
})
                                               If a /services/couchbase/ entry
                                               disappears or expires, then...
cbWatcher.on('change', event => {
  if (event.action === 'delete' || event.action === 'expire') {   ◁———
    if (event.prevNode.value === FIRST_NODE) {
      FIRST_NODE = etcd                         ◁————                ...if FIRST_NODE
        .getSync('services/couchbase', {recursive:true})            was the node that
        .body.node.nodes[0].value                                   was lost, reset
      console.log('FIRST_NODE lost, re-setting to:', FIRST_NODE)    FIRST_NODE to a
    }                                                               different etcd
    failNode(event.prevNode.value, msg => {     ◁————               element...
      rebalanceCluster()                        ◁————
      console.log('NODE LOST:', msg.toString())
    })                                                   ...run failNode() (listing 7.14)
  }                                                      on that IP, and...
})
                                                         ...rebalance the cluster.
cbConfigWatcher.on('delete', deletedConfig => {
  console.log('CONFIG DELETED, EXITING')        ◁——┐  If your config is deleted,
  process.exit(5)                                      exit the program.
})
```

You want to listen for new nodes and add them to the cluster, and you should also listen for removed nodes so you can remove them from the cluster. You also need to make sure conductor keeps working, so if you lose FIRST_NODE, you have to change it to something else. If you lose your configuration entirely, you need to exit, because that means you may be starting over from scratch.

Finally, you're at the program's entry point: executing `initCluster()`.

Listing 7.16 code/ch7/conductor/conductor.js: `initCluster()`

```
initCluster(msg => {
  console.log(msg)
  cb('setting-autofailover', FIRST_NODE, [          Enables Couchbase autofailover in
    '--auto-failover-timeout=30',                    case conductor fails for any reason
    '--enable-auto-failover=1'
  ]).stdout.on('data', afOut => {                    Waits 5 seconds, and runs
    setTimeout(initialAdd, 5000)                      initialAdd() (listing 7.12)
    console.log('autofailover set:', afOut.toString())
  })
})
```

Here, you enable Couchbase's autofailover feature, which will "hard failover" any node the cluster can't reach after a minimum of 30 seconds. It won't re-add nodes that become available again. You need this in case you lose the node on which conductor is running. If it takes more than 30 seconds for conductor to start up on another machine in your CoreOS cluster, Couchbase should still fail the data service on that node. As long as this timeout (30 seconds) is longer than your TTL for the key in etcd (if you remember, you set this to 8 seconds), this should also prevent any race conditions. After you ensure that this feature is on, you run the `initialAdd()` function after giving Couchbase 5 seconds to start up to kick off the entire cluster.

That's it! Pull all of these parts in a single file named conductor.js, and you can build your Docker image; or use mattbailey/ch7-conductor.

I've covered *a lot* of logic, and you can probably see why I didn't have you attempt this example in BASH. It's certainly possible in BASH—or in any language—and building orchestration programs like this will start to become your library of *infrastructure as code*. You'll iterate and improve on these programs just like any other software, and you'll be able to spin them up locally and test them in a variety of scenarios under Vagrant just as you'll do in the next sections.

7.2.3 *Startup and verification*

You've added a lot of moving parts to manage the persistence layer, so start it up and make sure it's running smoothly. Once your Vagrant cluster is ready, start up the services as you've done throughout this book. It's also useful to start watching conductor's journal:

```
$ fleetctl start code/ch7/couchbase@{1..3}.service \
  code/ch7/couchbase-sidekick@{1..3}.service \
  code/ch7/conductor/conductor.service
$ fleetctl journal -f conductor
```

As you can see, you start up three nodes for Couchbase and one for conductor. It doesn't matter which machine conductor runs on; it will float around the cluster when there are outages. It may take some time for the Docker images to download, but when they're ready, the output from conductor should look something like this:

Sets the default because conductor couldn't find any config

Conductor runs the cluster-init command first...   **...and then bucket-create...**

```
core-03 docker[2568]: no config, setting default:
  ➥{ password: 'Password1', nodes: 3, bucket: 'default', ram: 500 }
core-03 docker[2568]: LOADED CONFIG:
  ➥{ password: 'Password1', nodes: 3, bucket: 'default', ram: 500 }
core-03 docker[2568]: cluster-init: SUCCESS: init/edit 10.1.74.2
core-03 docker[2568]: bucket-create: SUCCESS: bucket-create
core-03 docker[2568]: autofailover set:
  ➥SUCCESS: set auto failover settings
core-03 docker[2568]: found other nodes: [ { key: '/services/couchbase/1',
core-03 docker[2568]:     value: '10.1.64.2',
core-03 docker[2568]:     expiration: '2016-05-29T04:27:34.017167896Z',
core-03 docker[2568]:     ttl: 7,
core-03 docker[2568]:     modifiedIndex: 3303,
core-03 docker[2568]:     createdIndex: 3249 },
core-03 docker[2568]:   { key: '/services/couchbase/3',
core-03 docker[2568]:     value: '10.1.13.2',
core-03 docker[2568]:     expiration: '2016-05-29T04:27:31.688554998Z',
core-03 docker[2568]:     ttl: 5,
core-03 docker[2568]:     modifiedIndex: 3301,
core-03 docker[2568]:     createdIndex: 3301 } ]
core-03 docker[2568]: attempting to add: 10.1.64.2
core-03 docker[2568]: attempting to add: 10.1.13.2
core-03 docker[2568]: [ 'SUCCESS: server-add 10.1.64.2:8091\n',
core-03 docker[2568]:   'SUCCESS: server-add 10.1.13.2:8091\n' ]
core-03 docker[2568]: INFO: rebalancing
core-03 docker[2568]: .
core-03 docker[2568]: SUCCESS: rebalanced cluster
```

...and sets the autofailover feature.

Conductor has found two other Couchbase nodes in etcd...

...so it attempts to add them to the cluster...

...and then rebalances.

You'll see a lot of dots being output while conductor is rebalancing, followed by (hopefully) this success message.

Your cluster should now be up and running with three nodes. You can check on any of the nodes in the cluster via their web control panels; the Server Nodes tab should look something like figure 7.2 earlier in the chapter.

Now that your robust distributed data store is up, in the next section, you'll start pushing data into it with your new workers.

7.2.4 *Starting your workers*

You should have everything you need to get these workers started. You've put the API keys into etcd, and the persistent store is ready to go. All you have to do is start up the service units. Let's start six instances of the worker. You'll still probably hit the API limit pretty quickly, but you want to see how this works and begin looking at one of the instances right away:

All the Couchbase nodes the
worker is connecting to

```
$ fleetctl start code/ch7/worker/worker@{1..6}.service && \
  fleetctl journal -f worker@1
...
Jun 01 02:51:28 core-01 docker[4846]: current connection:
  couchbase://10.1.69.2,10.1.42.2,10.1.74.2
Jun 01 02:51:29 core-01 docker[4846]: zag 15
Jun 01 02:51:29 core-01 docker[4846]: theism 15
...
Jun 01 02:51:32 core-01 docker[4846]: Twitter threw error:
  [ { message: 'Rate limit exceeded', code: 88 } ]
...
Jun 01 02:51:43 core-01 systemd[1]: Stopped Worker Service 1.
...
Jun 01 02:51:45 core-01 systemd[1]: Started Worker Service 1.
Jun 01 02:51:47 core-01 docker[5113]: lock engaged, exiting
```

Starts collecting search results. I got about 40 per worker in around 3 seconds until…

…Twitter rate-limited me.

The worker exits.

The service unit has a 10-second RestartSec, so it starts up again.

There's still a lock, so the worker quickly exits.

Here you can see the entire workflow of the worker: connecting to Couchbase, running and storing queries, exiting on rate limit, and then reacting to the distributed lock on restart. If you want to, you can check out another worker and see that it's reacting to the lock the same way. When this lock expires, in 15 minutes, the next worker to launch will begin gathering data again, and so on. You could conceivably run this forever.

Figure 7.3 shows how the database is doing. You now have a bunch of records in the three-node Couchbase cluster.

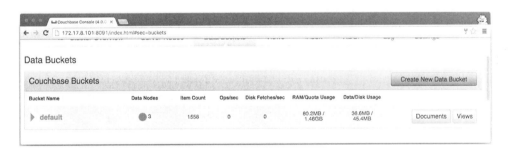

Figure 7.3 You have data.

If you go back and fire up the web app and memcached units from chapter 6, you can view the tweets as well. Figure 7.4 shows the same real-time data; if you happen to catch the log before the worker gets rate-limited by Twitter, you can also see it change on update.

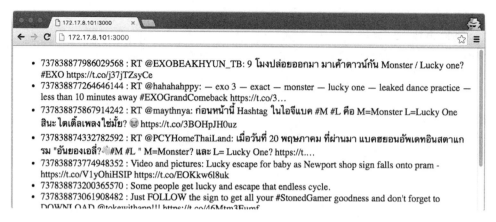

Figure 7.4   Browser view

Now you have a full stack with a backing database with a purpose, and clear lines of scalability and fault tolerance. Where do you go from here? It's time to break the stack, of course!

7.3   *Breaking your stack*

As always, we'll begin by simulating a node failure (on only one node, because you have only three nodes to work with) and then go through how to recover. This will be a little different: bringing the cluster back to a "green" state takes more processing power, because you're dealing with actual data that needs to be distributed. The larger your data set gets, the longer the redistribution of data takes. But most distributed data stores (Couchbase included) improve the speed of recovery as you increase the size of the cluster, so be sure you read up on how to plan this for the database you're using.

7.3.1   *Watching the failure*

It's a good idea to watch the conductor service while you do this, so you can see in real time what's happening. The conductor program is configured to move to a different machine if the one it's running on fails, so, for the purpose of this example, you should make sure you're shutting down one that isn't running it. You can, of course, experiment on your own, to see the time difference between the conductor machine failing and a different one; I encourage you to think about how you could get a conductor running on all nodes using a distributed lock.

Have Vagrant shut down a node, and watch conductor immediately after that:

```
$ vagrant halt core-01 && fleetctl journal -f conductor
==> core-01: Attempting graceful shutdown of VM...
...
Jun 01 03:25:38 core-03 docker[10041]:
➥NODE LOST: SUCCESS: failover ns_1@10.1.42.2
```

Conductor saw the service exit on etcd, so it issued a failover.

```
Jun 01 03:25:38 core-03 docker[10041]: INFO: rebalancing
...
Jun 01 03:26:07 core-03 docker[10041]: SUCCESS: rebalanced cluster
```

A rebalance was triggered.   **Successful rebalance**

As you can see, this took about 30 seconds to complete. The larger your dataset gets, the longer it will take for the cluster to rebalance. Also look at the journal for web@1. You can see that it restarted too, to update its Couchbase connections:

```
$ fleetctl journal -f web@1
...
Jun 01 03:25:55 core-03 docker[19917]:
➥current config: { couchbase: 'couchbase://10.1.74.2,10.1.69.2',
...
```

This should leave your users with very little downtime, even though you've had a fairly critical failure in one part of your system. Next, you'll bring the node back up and watch the same things happen to restore full service.

7.3.2 Restoring the machine

Do the same thing here—start up the instance, and immediately watch the conductor service:

As expected, conductor discovered the new node, added it, and rebalanced.

```
$ vagrant up core-01 && fleetctl journal -f conductor
Bringing machine 'core-01' up with 'virtualbox' provider...
...
Jun 01 03:33:53 core-03 docker[10041]: attempting to add: 10.1.42.3
Jun 01 03:33:55 core-03 docker[10041]:
➥Node added, rebalancing: SUCCESS: server-add 10.1.42.3:8091
Jun 01 03:34:01 core-03 docker[10041]: INFO: rebalancing
...
Jun 01 03:35:10 core-03 docker[10041]: SUCCESS: rebalanced cluster
```

Notice that it took more than a minute to rebalance the cluster on restoration. This is typical behavior, and it makes sense if you think about how rebalancing data operates. Usually, write I/O is the performance constraint on these operations. This is a simplistic explanation, but when a node leaves the cluster, the data has to be split and then written to *two* nodes, so the write load is distributed between them. When a node rejoins, that same volume of data needs to be written to *one* node. Even though these are VMs running on the same machine, the parallel operation is faster than the more serial one. The disparity will probably be even more obvious if you're using magnetic drives rather than solid-state drives.

You should now have a good understanding of how to build a Big Data platform on CoreOS. I encourage you to play around with settings in Couchbase and experiment with different scenarios.

7.4 *Summary*

- Do some research on the mechanics of how your chosen platform can scale. This will have a major impact on how easy or difficult it is to write orchestration programs.
- Always test failures on these systems before you go to production.
- I did *not* cover backups in this chapter, because Big Data archival methods can present unique problems.
- Know your data system's formula for replication and distribution, and how (if possible) you can change it.
- If you're doing data acquisition with workers, keep these tips in mind:
  - Initialize rapidly.
  - Store no state.
  - Fail fast.

Part 3

CoreOS in production

In chapters 8–10, you'll begin by spinning up a CoreOS cluster in Amazon Web Services. Next, you'll take the complex application you've built in your local sandbox, and automate its deployment to your cluster in AWS. Finally, I'll wrap up the book by presenting a general systems administration guide that covers some patterns for logging and backups, and I'll touch on what's on the horizon for CoreOS.

CoreOS on AWS

This chapter covers

- Supporting CoreOS with an AWS virtual infrastructure
- Building out scalable CoreOS on that infrastructure
- Attaching a dynamic load balancer to a cluster
- Deploying services with the AWS CLI

This chapter shifts away from application architecture and local development instances of CoreOS, and works through a production deployment of CoreOS in Amazon Web Services (AWS). We'll start small, with a simple cluster that looks similar to your development environment; then, we'll build out some more-complex infrastructures for performance and availability, scaling across different vectors.

By the end of this chapter, you'll have a scalable production platform on which you can run your applications; and in chapter 9, you'll work on deploying the application stack you've built in the last few chapters onto this infrastructure. You'll learn how to stand up a basic CoreOS cluster in AWS that spans availability zones and can act as a baseline for any application stack you want to build.

NOTE   This chapter doesn't require that you have strong AWS skills already, but I assume you can read some AWS documentation and get your account set up (see the requirements listed in section 8.1.3). The chapter may seem a little less dense, though, if you have some experience or have read literature such as Manning's *Amazon Web Services in Action* (Michael Wittig and Andreas Wittig, 2015, www.manning.com/books/amazon-web-services-in-action).

NOTE   The examples in this chapter involve running live services in AWS. Neither I nor Manning Publications is responsible for costs you'll incur by running these examples. You'll be using a pretty small amount of resources—about $1.00 to $2.00 per day if you forget to turn off the lights.

8.1   *AWS background*

As discussed in chapter 4, you have a lot of options when it comes to running CoreOS in a public (or private) cloud environment. All cloud deployments have their nuances, but AWS has been first to market with features in general and is the most commonly used platform. AWS is also well supported by CoreOS, and it gives you a lot of tools up front to get you started. This chapter will walk you through a production-ready CloudFormation template, explaining each part of how it's put together.

This section reviews some AWS terminology and looks at the top-level view of what you're going to build. You'll be using some advanced features of AWS, but we'll cover enough of the basic mechanics of these features that you don't need to be an expert in AWS. If you're interested in a more in-depth book on AWS, see *Amazon Web Services in Action.*

The goal of this chapter is to show you how to build a production infrastructure for the product you've created in the previous few chapters. Figure 8.1 shows a diagram of the end product: you'll build a high-availability setup across three availability zones, with an Auto Scaling group (ASG) to scale for capacity. You'll also use flannel's ability to be backed by the AWS VPC API. If you already have experience with AWS, you may be able to skip to section 8.2.

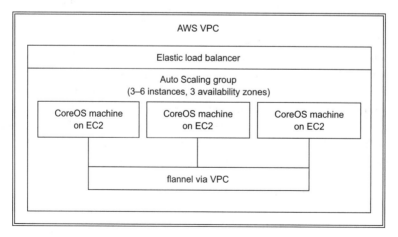

Figure 8.1   Infrastructure architecture

8.1.1 *AWS regions and uptimes*

AWS has a service-level agreement (SLA; https://aws.amazon.com/ec2/sla) that states it will make "commercially reasonable efforts" to maintain 99.95% uptime for EC2 (the virtual machine platform) and EBS (block storage for EC2) within a region. Each region has *availability zones* (us-west-2a, us-west-2b, and so on). AWS defines *downtime* (which it refers to as *Region Unavailable*) as more than one availability zone (AZ) within a region being unavailable. This means if you're not across more than one AZ, you can't ever guarantee an SLA for your customers. AWS does *not* have an SLA for a single AZ. If your architecture *is* cross-AZ (meaning it can survive an AZ outage for any period of time), the *highest* SLA you can claim for your customers is 99.95%, which translates to about 22 minutes of downtime allowed per month. It's also important to note that when AWS fails its SLA, you're issued a service credit; this likely won't cover the damage the downtime causes to your company or product.

> ## Cross-region deployment
>
> If you need more than 99.95% uptime, you must be cross-region as well as cross-AZ. As you can imagine, there's a significant cost in both runtime price and system complexity for such a configuration (and possible diminishing returns). I won't cover cross-region deployments in this book, because they require highly customized setups with virtual VPNs running on discrete instances—not to mention the huge complexity of managing persistent data cross-region where latency is high.
>
> AWS has no built-in model for cross-region communication, making any kind of automation difficult when you're using things like security groups. VPC peering connections only work within the same region; peering across regions is a "planned feature."

All that being said, AWS typically *exceeds* its SLA. The last Region Unavailable event occurred in 2014, and partial AZ outages are also rare. If your organization requires hard numbers, you can only depend on having an SLA *less than or equal to* what AWS has.

> ## ECS
>
> AWS has a new service called Elastic Container Service (ECS). As discussed briefly in chapter 4, ECS provides an AWS API method for running Docker containers. With CoreOS, fleet can control services via that API. Of course, this adds significant complexity to the infrastructure. I won't cover this option in the scenario here for the sake of simplicity and so that you can focus on a single complete implementation.

8.1.2 *AWS services*

Your deployment into AWS will use a number of services, all deployed via a Cloud-Formation template as the primary tool you'll use to test, build, and make changes to your infrastructure. CloudFormation allows you to define (in YAML) a template for a complete implementation of anything in AWS. The AWS web console GUI is great and always getting better, but writing CloudFormation templates lets you keep your infrastructure in a known state and under source control. If you build things with the console GUI, how you did so (especially for complex systems) is quickly forgotten and difficult to reproduce. CloudFormation lets you design the entire layout and is absolutely the best practice for deploying any system into AWS.

This template will build out a virtual private cloud (VPC), which gives you a lot of control over the networking of your systems; you'll also take advantage of flannel's ability to use VPC as a back end for its network abstraction. Your template will define a set of permissions using AWS Identity and Access Management (IAM) to allow your CoreOS instances to perform a secure subset of AWS API actions; this is a requirement for flannel backed by the VPC API to function.

Finally, your CloudFormation template will cover elastic load balancers (ELBs) in each VPC in each region, to load-balance incoming connections to the services running on CoreOS across AZs. You'll also set up an empty S3 bucket that you'll use for backups in chapter 10.

8.1.3   Chapter requirements

The following sections jump right into setting up your infrastructure. Here's what you'll need to get started:

- An activated AWS account (you can create one at https://console.aws.amazon.com)
- AWS access key ID and secret access key for your account (see http://mng .bz/j0PP)
- The following tools installed on your workstation:
  - AWS CLI (http://mng.bz/N8L6)
  - SSH key-pair from EC2 (http://mng.bz/34ih)

8.1.4   CloudFormation template

As with other large listings in this book, I've split the template into a few parts and will discuss them as I go. Start a new YAML file called ch8-cfn-cluster.yml. This is loosely based on the example template provided by CoreOS, of which you can always find the latest version at http://mng.bz/6fUO. This chapter's version deviates significantly in the custom VPC setup and represents a much more real-world production implementation, rather than a simple example (you'll also use YAML instead of JSON, for readability).

Let's start with the boilerplate CloudFormation items and then break down the resources by VPC, security groups, IAM role, Auto Scaling group, load balancer, and S3 bucket. This is *a lot* to type in, if you're copying from the book, and probably error prone if you're pasting from the digital copy, so I recommend using the file from the book's code repository at www.manning.com/books/coreos-in-action (code/ch8/ch8-cfn-cluster.yml). Don't skip reading this section, though; you'll need to be familiar with the parts of this file later.

  This template will ultimately provide you with enough boilerplate configuration to build any CoreOS system in AWS. You'll continue to work on it in chapters 9 and 10.

MAPS, PARAMETERS, AND OUTPUTS

You'll use four top-level objects (not including the description string) in this Cloud-Formation file: `Mappings`, `Parameters`, and `Outputs` are covered in this subsection, and `Resources` will be further broken down. Start your file with the following data (code/ch8/ch8-cfn-cluster.yml).

Listing 8.1 Metadata

```
Mappings:                                      This mapping contains the official
  RegionMap:                                   CoreOS AMIs per region (at the time
    us-west-2:                                 of writing; this changes often, but
      AMI: ami-7d11c51d                        older ones will always work).
      a: 10.1.1.0/24                           Subnet mappings per AZ in a region,
      b: 10.1.2.0/24                           as well as the VPC network block
      c: 10.1.3.0/24
      VPC: 10.1.0.0/16
Parameters:                                    Friendly input to change
  InstanceType:                                the instance type
    Description: EC2 HVM instance type (t2.small, etc).
    Type: String
    Default: t2.small
    ConstraintDescription: Must be a valid EC2 HVM instance type.   Input to change
  DiscoveryURL:                                                     the discovery URL
    Description: An unique etcd cluster discovery URL.
Grab a new token from https://discovery.etcd.io/new?size=<your cluster size>
    Type: String
  AllowSSHFrom:                                                  Input to change
    Description: The net block (CIDR) that SSH is available to.  the IPs allowed to
    Default: 0.0.0.0/0                                           ssh to your cluster
    Type: String
  KeyPair:
    Description: The name of an EC2 Key Pair to allow
      SSH access to the instance.                            Input to set the SSH key
    Type: AWS::EC2::KeyPair::KeyName                         for your instances
    MinLength: 1
Outputs:                                          Output to show you the ELB
  ELB:                                            hostname that will be created
    Description: ELB Hostname
    Value: !GetAtt [ LoadBalancer, DNSName ]
  Backup:                                         Output to show you the S3
    Description: S3 Bucket for Backups            bucket name for the backup
    Value: !Ref S3Backup                          bucket that will be created
```

`Mappings` is an object to map out relative parameters to some variable. Usually, this is so you can maintain a single CloudFormation template with multiple purposes (such as multiple regions). `Parameters` is a place for user input that you can reference in the template (you'll see later how this works).

If you want to fetch the latest CoreOS Amazon Machine Image (AMI) number for `RegionMap`, you can find it at http://mng.bz/6fUO. To be clear, you don't have to change this all the time; CoreOS will do its auto-upgrade procedure from any image. I've provided mappings for us-east-1 and us-west-2 for the sake of brevity; you can add more if you like. The IP networks are arbitrary: the only caveat is that they must not overlap per AZ, and they must not overlap whatever you plan to use for flannel.

The input parameters should be self-explanatory, except for `DiscoveryURL`. Vagrant managed creating this token for you automatically, but for this example, you have to go to https://discovery.etcd.io/new. Then, paste the URL it generates as the parameter (when you execute this template). If you wipe out your cluster in AWS, you'll have to generate a new one of these token URLs each time.

The `Outputs` section emits useful data about your cluster. If you want to add to this (or anything else), you can read the CloudFormation development docs at http://mng.bz/27ww.

Now, let's get into the resources, starting with the VPC and network configuration.

VPC AND NETWORK CONFIGURATION

This section looks like a lot of detailed information, but most of it involves setting up the different components of a VPC with their default settings for three AZs. You'll define the basic networking components of the VPC and essentially set up the virtual layer 3 configuration of your private cloud. Figure 8.2 shows what you're building for the network topology.

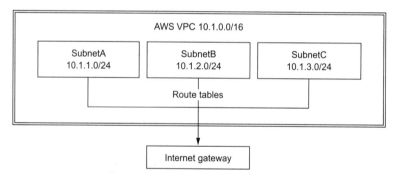

Figure 8.2   Network topology

As you can see, you're setting up three /24 network segments, configuring their route tables so they can communicate with each other, and attaching them all to an internet gateway. This is all standard VPC configuration that you'd see in most CloudFormation templates. To split up these boilerplate resources, let's start with the ones that don't specify an AZ (code/ch8/ch8-cfn-cluster.yml).

Listing 8.2 VPC 1

```
Resources:
  VPC:                          ◁——— Creates the base VPC object in AWS
    Type: AWS::EC2::VPC
    Properties:
      CidrBlock: !FindInMap [ RegionMap, !Ref "AWS::Region", VPC ]    ◁
      InstanceTenancy: default
      EnableDnsSupport: true
      EnableDnsHostnames: true
  InternetGateway:              ◁········ Internet gateway router
    Type: AWS::EC2::InternetGateway
    Properties: {}
  AttachGateway:                ◁——— Attaches the router to your VPC
    Type: AWS::EC2::VPCGatewayAttachment
    Properties:
      VpcId: !Ref VPC
      InternetGatewayId: !Ref InternetGateway
  RouteTable:                   ◁
    Type: AWS::EC2::RouteTable
    Properties: { VpcId: !Ref VPC }
  InternetEgressRoute:          ◁
    Type: AWS::EC2::Route
    DependsOn: AttachGateway
    Properties:
      RouteTableId: !Ref RouteTable
      DestinationCidrBlock: 0.0.0.0/0
      GatewayId: !Ref InternetGateway
  InternetNetworkAcl:           ◁——— Creates the default ACL
    Type: AWS::EC2::NetworkAcl
    Properties: { VpcId: !Ref VPC }
```

Everything is default except this, which you defined in the Mappings settings in listing 8.1.

Initializes the default route table

Sets the default route to the gateway router

The VPC, gateway, basic routes, and ACL are finished. The next listing shows the subnet configuration with three subnets, one for each AZ (code/ch8/ch8-cfn-cluster.yml).

Listing 8.3 VPC 2

```
SubnetA:                              Uses the subnet mappings (listing 8.1)
  Type: AWS::EC2::Subnet                   to set the subnet network
  Properties:
    CidrBlock: !FindInMap [ RegionMap, !Ref "AWS::Region", a ]    ◁
    AvailabilityZone: !Sub ${AWS::Region}a
    VpcId: !Ref VPC
SubnetB:
  Type: AWS::EC2::Subnet
  Properties:
    CidrBlock: !FindInMap [ RegionMap, !Ref "AWS::Region", b ]
    AvailabilityZone: !Sub ${AWS::Region}b
    VpcId: !Ref VPC
SubnetC:
  Type: AWS::EC2::Subnet
  Properties:
    CidrBlock: !FindInMap [ RegionMap, !Ref "AWS::Region", c ]
    AvailabilityZone: !Sub ${AWS::Region}c
```

```
        VpcId: !Ref VPC                                    Associates the subnets
  AssociationSubnetA:                          ◁──────┘    to the route table
    Type: AWS::EC2::SubnetRouteTableAssociation
    Properties: { SubnetId: !Ref SubnetA, RouteTableId: !Ref RouteTable }
  AssociationSubnetB:
    Type: AWS::EC2::SubnetRouteTableAssociation
    Properties: { SubnetId: !Ref SubnetB, RouteTableId: !Ref RouteTable }
  AssociationSubnetC:
    Type: AWS::EC2::SubnetRouteTableAssociation
    Properties: { SubnetId: !Ref SubnetC, RouteTableId: !Ref RouteTable }
```

As you can see, you build out one subnet for each AZ and then ensure that their routes are configured. You use the earlier mappings to define the network CIDR. This represents all the basic VPC setup; let's move on to the IAM instance profile and security groups.

IAM AND SECURITY GROUPS

IAM provides a standard, flexible way to securely grant access to EC2 (known as the *Principal* element), so that you can perform actions on AWS resources. In listing 8.4 (code/ch8/ch8-cfn-cluster.yml), you'll create the security group that lets you perform certain actions on the AWS API *from within the instance.* This is a requirement for flannel so that it can create and modify the VPC route tables and so that you can disable the source/destination check on the EC2 instance. This modification is necessary because flannel will be communicating from an IP other than the one assigned by the subnet.

Listing 8.4   IAM

```
CoreOSRole:                        ◁───┐  Creates a role to put
    Type: AWS::IAM::Role               │  your policies in
    Properties:
      AssumeRolePolicyDocument:
        Version: 2012-10-17
        Statement:
          - Effect: Allow
            Principal: { Service: [ ec2.amazonaws.com ] }
            Action: [ "sts:AssumeRole" ]
      Path: /
      Policies:
        - PolicyName: coreos
          PolicyDocument:
            Version: 2012-10-17
            Statement:                          Set of permissions
              - Effect: Allow                   that lets flannel
                Action:                         change the VPC config
                  - "ec2:CreateRoute"
                  - "ec2:DeleteRoute"                        These next two
                  - "ec2:ReplaceRoute"                       actions allow you to
                  - "ec2:ModifyNetworkInterfaceAttribute"    disable the
                  - "ec2:ModifyInstanceAttribute"            source/dest check.
                Resource: "*"
              - Effect: Allow
                Action: [ "ec2:DescribeRouteTables",
```

```
            ➡"ec2:DescribeInstances" ]
               Resource: "*"
CoreOSInstanceProfile:
  Type: AWS::IAM::InstanceProfile
  DependsOn: [ CoreOSRole ]
  Properties:
    Path: /
    Roles: [ !Ref CoreOSRole ]
```

These two actions are so that flannel can inspect the state of the routes.

Creates an EC2 instance profile attached to the role you'll associate with your instances

This code looks complicated—IAM roles have a lot of nested objects—but it's fairly basic and pulled from a combination of the CloudFormation documentation and the flannel VPC-backend documentation at https://coreos.com/flannel/docs/latest/aws-vpc-backend.html. The IAM role you're creating here becomes attached to instance profiles (which are then associated with EC2 instances), which will grant permission for software running on these instances to perform actions on EC2. The actions granted manipulate network routes and interfaces. This is usually preferable to passing around AWS API keys, because you don't have to manage or secure these secrets in any other tool.

IAM roles are important components to learn for building stacks that have complex interactions or integrations with AWS. They're your keys to managing AWS features in an automated way from within AWS.

Next, you can define your security groups and their ingress definitions (code/ch8/ch8-cfn-cluster.yml).

Listing 8.5 Security groups

```
ELBSecurityGroup:
    Type: AWS::EC2::SecurityGroup
    Properties:
      GroupDescription: LoadBalancer SecurityGroup
      VpcId: !Ref VPC
      SecurityGroupIngress:
        - { IpProtocol: tcp, FromPort: 80, ToPort:
      ➡80, CidrIp: 0.0.0.0/0 }
        - { IpProtocol: tcp, FromPort: 8091,
      ➡ToPort: 8091, CidrIp: 0.0.0.0/0 }
  CoreOSSecurityGroup:
    Type: AWS::EC2::SecurityGroup
    DependsOn: [ ELBSecurityGroup ]
    Properties:
      GroupDescription: CoreOS SecurityGroup
      VpcId: !Ref VPC
      SecurityGroupIngress:
        - { IpProtocol: tcp, FromPort: 22,
      ➡ToPort: 22, CidrIp: !Ref AllowSSHFrom }
        - { IpProtocol: -1, CidrIp: 10.10.0.0/16 }
        - { IpProtocol: -1, SourceSecurityGroupId:
      ➡!Ref ELBSecurityGroup }
```

Security group you'll use for the load balancer

You want the world to access this load balancer (you can scope this down if you want).

You can leave this open for testing, but this is your Couchbase admin panel.

Security group for the CoreOS cluster

Opens SSH to the network you specified in Properties

Allows traffic from flannel

Allows all incoming traffic from the load balancer

The next listing adds a few discrete ingress rules (code/ch8/ch8-cfn-cluster.yml).

Listing 8.6   Security group ingress rules

```
Ingress4001:                                    ◄─────────     The rest of these ingress rules
    Type: AWS::EC2::SecurityGroupIngress                       are for internal communication
    DependsOn: [ CoreOSSecurityGroup ]                         between fleet, etcd, and flannel.
    Properties:
      GroupId: !GetAtt [ CoreOSSecurityGroup, GroupId ]
      IpProtocol: tcp
      FromPort: 4001
      ToPort: 4001
      SourceSecurityGroupId: !GetAtt [ CoreOSSecurityGroup, GroupId ]
  Ingress2379:
    Type: AWS::EC2::SecurityGroupIngress
    DependsOn: [ CoreOSSecurityGroup ]
    Properties:
      GroupId: !GetAtt [ CoreOSSecurityGroup, GroupId ]
      IpProtocol: tcp
      FromPort: 2379
      ToPort: 2379
      SourceSecurityGroupId: !GetAtt [ CoreOSSecurityGroup, GroupId ]
  Ingress2380:
    Type: AWS::EC2::SecurityGroupIngress
    DependsOn: [ CoreOSSecurityGroup ]
    Properties:
      GroupId: !GetAtt [ CoreOSSecurityGroup, GroupId ]
      IpProtocol: tcp
      FromPort: 2380
      ToPort: 2380
      SourceSecurityGroupId: !GetAtt [ CoreOSSecurityGroup, GroupId ]
```

Normally, with security groups, you add ingress rules to the `SecurityGroupIngress` property list when you create the security group. But to add ingress rules *from* a security group *to* the same security group, you have to define them separately from the group, as in this listing. This is to prevent a chicken-and-egg scenario, because the security group can't reference before it's created; you'll notice that each of the discrete ingress rules depends on the group being created first.

All of your communication settings are configured. Everything should be able to talk to what it needs to, with a high level of security. At this point, you've completed the networking configuration for your stack.

> **NOTE** It's common, either by way of policy or for your own sense of organization, to break this configuration out into its own CloudFormation stack. We won't break this apart here, but the template up to this point might be owned by an infrastructure team, whereas the remainder of the template might be broken into a new stack for a development team, so they can be iterated on separately.

Next you'll (finally!) get into the actual CoreOS cluster deployment, which is where you'll build out the resources that depend on the infrastructure created thus far in the template.

AUTO SCALING GROUP

You'll set up a simple ASG with a static size of three nodes for your CoreOS cluster (we'll cover more-dynamic scaling in chapter 10). ASGs in CloudFormation consist of two objects: the ASG, which tells where the group hooks up and how many instances to create; and a *launch configuration* that tells AWS how each VM should function. The ASG and associated launch configuration together define how a cluster of EC2 compute resources behave in AWS in the following ways:

- Which VPC subnets the ASG can launch EC2 instances in
- How many instances are in the cluster
- What load balancers should automatically add the instances to their targets
- What EC2 machine image to use
- Normal EC2 configuration for all the instances in the ASG (such as instance type, block storage, and SSH key)
- What the user data is for initial configuration and bootstrapping

First, let's look at the ASG (code/ch8/ch8-cfn-cluster.yml).

Listing 8.7 `AutoScaleGroup`

```
CoreOSServerAutoScale:
    Type: AWS::AutoScaling::AutoScalingGroup
    DependsOn: [ VPC, WebTargetGroup, CouchbaseTargetGroup ]
    Properties:
      VPCZoneIdentifier: [ !Ref SubnetA, !Ref SubnetB, !Ref SubnetC ]
      LaunchConfigurationName: !Ref CoreOSServerLaunchConfig
      MinSize: 3
      MaxSize: 3
      DesiredCapacity: 3
      LoadBalancerNames: [ !Ref InternalEtcdLB ]
      TargetGroupARNs: [ !Ref WebTargetGroup, !Ref CouchbaseTargetGroup ]
```

Reference to the launch configuration (see listing 8.8)

Associated VPC subnets

Min and max cluster size (remember, etcd needs at least three)

Creates an attachment to the classic load balancer for etcd

*CloudFormation stack won't enter a **CREATE_COMPLETE** state until you have at least this many nodes up.*

Creates attachments to target groups for ELBv2 load balancers for both the web app and the Couchbase admin panel

---

You have two types of load-balancer attachments. `InternalEtcdLB` could also be a v2 ELB, but I've used the classic one here to demonstrate both options. `TargetGroupARNs` are targets for ELBv2, and they're new (and great: they support WebSockets and HTTP/2). The goal for both of these properties is the same, though: you want `AutoScaleGroup` to automatically associate its instances with these load-balancer resources.

NOTE   The full load-balancer definitions are in the next subsection.

Now for the launch configuration (code/ch8/ch8-cfn-cluster.yml).

Listing 8.8   Launch configuration

References the
InstanceType specified
in Parameters

```
CoreOSServerLaunchConfig:
    DependsOn: [ VPC, CoreOSSecurityGroup, CoreOSInstanceProfile ]
    Type: AWS::AutoScaling::LaunchConfiguration
    Properties:
      ImageId: !FindInMap [ RegionMap, !Ref "AWS::Region", AMI ]
      InstanceType: !Ref InstanceType
      KeyName: !Ref KeyPair
      SecurityGroups: [ !Ref CoreOSSecurityGroup ]
      IamInstanceProfile: !Ref CoreOSInstanceProfile
      AssociatePublicIpAddress: true
      BlockDeviceMappings:
        - DeviceName: /dev/xvdb
          Ebs: { VolumeSize: 10, VolumeType:
            gp2, DeleteOnTermination: true }
      UserData:
        "Fn::Base64": !Sub |
```

References the
AMI specified
in Mappings

References
the SSH key
specified in
Parameters

Attaches to the IAM
profile created in the
last section

Not all instances need drive
attachments, but all the
cheap t2 ones do.

This is the hard part: your
cloud-config, which gets
Base64-encoded.

Make sure you give a public IP, so you can
ssh to it (this also becomes the egress IP).

Attaches to the CoreOSSecurityGroup
created in the last section

Let's go through this in more depth, because this is where things get interesting. We'll ignore the content of UserData for the time being; but UserData is where CoreOS will look for its cloud-config, so it will be a large YAML file that you have to encode. In AWS CloudFormation, every property of a resource has an associated update requirement. The AWS documentation on UserData (http://mng.bz/8th9) shows "*Update requires:* Replacement." This means if you change cloud-config in UserData, the configuration of the instances that are already launched will *not* be changed. If you want to update their cloud-config, they must be terminated and re-created. This also means everything about your cluster will be destroyed if you do this, so cloud-config should be generic. Further, if you end up changing it, you must be sure to generate a new discovery token so you can initialize a new cluster.

We'll get into the cloud-config you're using for this cluster later in the chapter, so remember this UserData spot in the file. For now, let's finish the template with the load balancers and S3 bucket.

ELBs AND S3

In listing 8.9, you create a simple ELB for external access to the application you'll deploy, and an internal ELB that you'll use in chapter 9 to talk to etcd from other AWS services (code/ch8/ch8-cfn-cluster.yml). These are both referenced in the ASG. You also deploy an S3 bucket and policy that you'll use in chapter 10 for backups. You're using the newer ELBv2 type, because it plays more nicely with the WebSockets in the example application. Within that ELB, you make a listener for both your web app and the Couchbase admin panel. Normally, you might split these up more for security, but for the sake of brevity, this example keeps them in the same ELB.

Listing 8.9 ELBv2 base

```
LoadBalancer:
    Type: AWS::ElasticLoadBalancingV2::LoadBalancer
    DependsOn: [ ELBSecurityGroup ]              The base ELBv2 needs to
    Properties:                                   define its security group...
      SecurityGroups: [ !Ref ELBSecurityGroup ]  ◁
      Subnets: [ !Ref SubnetA, !Ref SubnetB, !Ref SubnetC ]  ◁── ...and VPC subnets.
```

This is just the initial resource for the ELB. On its own, it doesn't do a lot; it needs listeners to expose to the internet, and target groups to know where to send connections.

Define the web target group and listener first (which will point to your node.js application; code/ch8/ch8-cfn-cluster.yml).

Listing 8.10 ELBv2 web app

```
WebTargetGroup:
    Type: AWS::ElasticLoadBalancingV2::TargetGroup   The target for the web app
    Properties:                                       runs on port 3000...
      Port: 3000                           ◁
      VpcId: !Ref VPC                      ◁────── ...and the targets live in your VPC.
      Protocol: HTTP
      TargetGroupAttributes:
        - { Key: stickiness.enabled, Value: true }  ◁    You need stickiness
        - { Key: stickiness.type, Value: lb_cookie }     for WebSockets to
  WebListener:                                            function correctly.
    Type: AWS::ElasticLoadBalancingV2::Listener
    DependsOn: [ LoadBalancer, WebTargetGroup ]          Attaches the
    Properties:                                          forwarding action
      DefaultActions: [ { Type: forward, TargetGroupArn:  to the target group
      ➥!Ref WebTargetGroup } ]            ◁
      Port: 80                                            
      LoadBalancerArn: !Ref LoadBalancer   ◁──── Attaches to the load balancer
      Protocol: HTTP
```
Listens on port 80

This listing creates a TCP port 80 listener on the load balancer, configured to balance across targets on port 3000 (the node.js application port).

Next, you'll make a load balancer to get to your Couchbase admin panel (code/ch8/ch8-cfn-cluster.yml).

Listing 8.11   ELBv2 Couchbase admin panel

```
CouchbaseTargetGroup:
   Type: AWS::ElasticLoadBalancingV2::TargetGroup
   Properties:
      Port: 8091                              The target for the Couchbase
      VpcId: !Ref VPC                         admin runs on port 8091.
      Protocol: HTTP
      TargetGroupAttributes:
         - { Key: stickiness.enabled, Value: true }
         - { Key: stickiness.type, Value: lb_cookie }
 CouchbaseListener:
   Type: AWS::ElasticLoadBalancingV2::Listener
   DependsOn: [ LoadBalancer, CouchbaseTargetGroup ]
   Properties:
      DefaultActions: [ { Type: forward, TargetGroupArn:
      ➥!Ref CouchbaseTargetGroup } ]
      Port: 8091                              Listens on port 8091
      LoadBalancerArn: !Ref LoadBalancer
      Protocol: HTTP
```

For the admin panel, you listen on port 8091 and load-balance to the same port on the targets.

For the internal etcd load balancer, you'll use the classic load balancer; this will let you talk to etcd without having to know anything about the hosts in the cluster, from within the VPC (code/ch8/ch8-cfn-cluster.yml). Essentially, this is a convenience for not having to programmatically discover a host to connect to for services not in the CoreOS cluster, such as AWS Lambda.

Listing 8.12   ELB (internal)

```
InternalEtcdLB:
   Type: AWS::ElasticLoadBalancing::LoadBalancer
   DependsOn: [ CoreOSSecurityGroup ]
   Properties:                            This means this ELB can only be accessed
      Scheme: internal                    from within the VPC, on local IPs.

      Listeners: [ { LoadBalancerPort: 2379,
      ➥InstancePort: 2379, Protocol: TCP } ]      Default port for etcd
      HealthCheck:
         Target: TCP:2379
         HealthyThreshold: 3
         UnhealthyThreshold: 5
         Interval: 10                             You want this tied to
         Timeout: 5                               the default internal
      SecurityGroups: [ !Ref CoreOSSecurityGroup ]    security group.
      Subnets: [ !Ref SubnetA, !Ref SubnetB, !Ref SubnetC ]
```

Now for the S3 backups bucket (code/ch8/ch8-cfn-cluster.yml).

Listing 8.13 S3 bucket

```
S3Backup:                    ⟵──── Creates the bucket
    Type: AWS::S3::Bucket                              Adds a rule to delete any
    Properties:                                        objects older than 10 days
      LifecycleConfiguration:
        Rules: [ { ExpirationInDays: 10, Status: Enabled } ]   ⟵
  BackupPolicy:              ⟵
    Type: AWS::S3::BucketPolicy         Creates your
    DependsOn: [ CoreOSRole ]           permissions policy
    Properties:
      Bucket: !Ref S3Backup
      PolicyDocument:
        Id: backup
        Version: 2012-10-17
        Statement:
          - Sid: backup                    The CoreOS instance profile role
            Action: "s3:*"                         should have access to...
            Effect: Allow
            Principal: { AWS: !GetAtt [ CoreOSRole, Arn ] }   ⟵
            Resource: [ !Sub "arn:aws:s3:::${S3Backup}",
            ➥ !Sub "arn:aws:s3:::${S3Backup}/*" ]  ⟵─┐ ...write to the bucket
                                                        and any object in it.
```

Notice that you set up an S3 bucket with a policy to allow the CoreOS nodes to do anything to this bucket. So, you can use it via its API without providing keys, the same way the IAM role allows you to perform EC2 actions from within the cluster.

Other than adding cloud-config via user data, this CloudFormation template is functionally complete:

- The base networking, routing, and port-based security groups are all in place.
- You've configured your compute resources to fit into that base platform.
- You've configured your external-edge load balancers, internal load balancer, and backup storage.

If you don't have much AWS experience, this should also give you a cursory understanding of how the different resource in AWS fit together. We'll get into cloud-config next, so that you can paste it in and get your cluster running!

8.1.5 *Cloud-config in AWS*

Let's look at where you are. Before we jump into cloud-config, take a look at figure 8.3; it shows all the infrastructure and resources you've defined and configured so far. Fortunately, with the new addition of the !Sub function in CloudFormation (see http://mng.bz/9D9L), it recently became a lot easier to drop the YAML-formatted cloud-config into a CloudFormation template as user data—especially one where you have to insert references to resources in the template. This was even harder if you weren't using YAML for your CloudFormation template, which is also a recent feature.

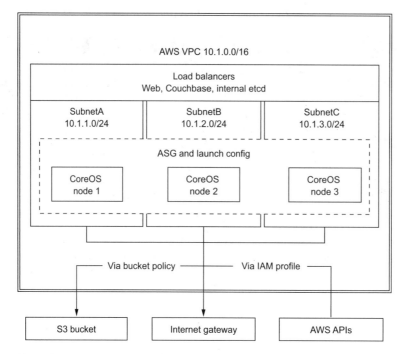

Figure 8.3   Infrastructure architecture

All of this cloud-config should fall under the `!Sub |` part of the ASG launch configuration in section 8.2.4. If in doubt, download the template referenced at the beginning of the chapter.

BOILERPLATE

The basic cloud-config for AWS is shown in the following listing.

Listing 8.14   Basic cloud-config

```
#cloud-config
coreos:
  etcd2:
    discovery: ${DiscoveryURL}                                    ◁─── etcd discovery URL from the
    advertise-client-urls: http://$private_ipv4:2379                   parameters at the beginning
    initial-advertise-peer-urls: http://$private_ipv4:2380             of the template
    listen-client-urls: http://0.0.0.0:2379,http://0.0.0.0:4001
    listen-peer-urls: http://$private_ipv4:2380
units:
  - name: etcd2.service
    command: start
  - name: fleet.service
    command: start
```

This should be similar to the `UserData` from Vagrant, way back at the beginning of the book. Here's an example of how this should *actually* look in your template in the ASG launch configuration:

```
...
    UserData:
      "Fn::Base64": !Sub |        ◁─────  This intrinsic function does a
        #cloud-config      ◁              Base64 encoding and uses the !Sub
        coreos:                            function to create a template.
          etcd2:                    The rest is the cloud-config you started
...                                 in listing 8.14 and will continue with.
```

With that explanation and the boilerplate cloud-config out of the way, you can continue with the rest of the unit definitions in cloud-config.

CUSTOM UNITS

The unit definitions in listing 8.15 should be appended under the basic cloud-config from listing 8.14. These are all the extra units to make things completely functional on boot, including flannel.

Listing 8.15   cloud-config.yml unit—metadata

```
- name: set-metadata.service
    runtime: true
    command: start
    content: |
      [Unit]
      Description=Puts metadata in /etc/instance        Puts instance id, AZ, and
      [Service]                                          region in /etc/instance
      Type=oneshot                                       as env vars
      RemainAfterExit=yes
      ExecStart=/usr/bin/sh -c 'echo INSTANCEID=$(curl http://169.254.169.254/
      ▰latest/meta-data/instance-id) > /etc/instance'    ◁
      ExecStart=/usr/bin/sh -c 'echo AZ=$(curl http://169.254.169.254/
      ▰latest/meta-data/placement/availability-zone) >> /etc/instance'
      ExecStart=/usr/bin/sh -c 'echo REGION=$(curl http://169.254.169.254/
      ▰latest/meta-data/placement/availability-zone
      ▰| rev | cut -c 2- | rev) >> /etc/instance'
```

This one-shot service is entirely for convenience later, so you don't have to query this information all the time. From within an AWS instance, you can always hit the http://169.254.169.254/latest/meta-data/ URL to get some information about the context in which that instance is running; the details on this API are at http://mng .bz/NvRT.

The next two units format and mount the filesystem for Docker. This is the 10 GB EBS device you added in the ASG launch configuration. You want to make sure this all happens before Docker starts.

Listing 8.16   cloud-config.yml unit—Docker filesystem

```
- name: format-docker.service
      runtime: true
      command: start
      content: |
        [Unit]
        Description=Wipe Ephemeral              You want this to format
        Before=docker.service          ◁────┘  early in the boot process.
        Before=docker-early.service
        [Service]                                        Wipes the drive you
        Type=oneshot                                     created in the launch
        RemainAfterExit=yes                              configuration...
        ExecStart=/usr/sbin/wipefs -f /dev/xvdb  ◁───┘
        ExecStart=/usr/sbin/mkfs.ext4 -m0 -L
        ➥docker -b 4096 -i 4096 -I 128 /dev/xvdb  ◁────
  - name: var-lib-docker.mount                          ...formats it
      command: start                                    with ext4...
      content: |
        [Unit]
        Description=Mount storage to /var/lib/docker
        Requires=format-docker.service
        After=format-docker.service
        Before=docker.service
        Before=docker-early.service
        [Mount]                          ...and mounts it to where
        What=/dev/xvdb          ◁────┘   Docker stores its data.
        Where=/var/lib/docker
        Type=ext4
```

The following unit starts flannel automatically on your instances and configures it to use a /16 network via the AWS VPC flannel driver. As a result, you should have zero overhead from using flannel.

Listing 8.17   cloud-config.yml unit—flannel

```
- name: flanneld.service
      command: start          ◁────── Starts flannel
      drop-ins:
        - name: 50-network-config.conf
          content: |
            [Service]
            ExecStartPre=/usr/bin/etcdctl set /coreos.com/network/config
            ➥'{ "Network": "10.10.0.0/16", "Backend":
            ➥{"Type": "aws-vpc"} }'
```

Sets the network for flannel, and tells it to use the aws-vpc back end

We discussed that flannel requires you turn of the source-dest check on the instances. Unfortunately (to date), AWS hasn't created a CloudFormation key to switch that off in an ASG. You can do it if you're spinning up discrete EC2 instances, but not in autoscale. That's why you have to create this last service (listing 8.18). The exact timing of running it is a bit hairy because you can only use the AWS CLI tools via a Docker container, and you're also messing around with Docker on boot, formatting its drive and making flannel start. The `source-dest` check doesn't have to be on for flannel to *start*—just for it to *function*—so it's okay if it waits until everything else is finished.

Listing 8.18   cloud-config.yml unit: `source-dest` check

```
- name: set-sdcheck-off.service
    runtime: true
    command: start
    content: |
      [Unit]
      Requires=var-lib-docker.mount
      ⇒ set-metadata.service flanneld.service
      After=var-lib-docker.mount set-metadata.service flanneld.service
      Description=Sets source-dest check to off
      [Service]
      EnvironmentFile=/etc/instance
      Type=oneshot
      RemainAfterExit=yes
      ExecStart=/usr/bin/docker run cgswong/aws:aws
      ⇒ --region $REGION ec2 modify-instance-attribute
      ⇒ --no-source-dest-check --instance-id $INSTANCEID
```

> **You want this to run after the metadata service, Docker formatting, and flannel have finished.**

> **Uses the /etc/instance environment file you created in the first one-shot**

> **Runs the AWS CLI tool to turn off the source-dest check on this instance**

This is a fairly generic baseline for cloud-config in AWS, and it should give you an understanding of the few extra bootstrapping procedures you need CoreOS to do to get the most out of running in AWS. Once this cloud-config YAML subdocument is finished and inserted with the appropriate indentation in your template, you should be ready to deploy the CloudFormation stack!

8.1.6   *Deployment*

You're finally ready to start up your CloudFormation stack. As a reminder: when you do this, the money clock starts running in AWS. I'll only cover deployment with the CLI, but the web console is pretty easy to work with. In both cases, you can reference either the file you've painstakingly assembled from this text or the file from the book's code repository.

In this section, you'll get a basic understanding of how to deploy and interact with all the infrastructure you've defined in the CloudFormation template in this chapter. The procedure is similar to any other CloudFormation stack you might create on your own, and this will be the stack you use for the rest of the book.

EXECUTION AND PARAMETERS

To start the deployment, you'll need the following as input parameters:

- A catchy name for your stack
- An IP in CIDR notation for SSH access (or 0.0.0.0/0)
- A new discovery URL (you can generate one at https://discovery.etcd.io/new)
- The instance type you want (see https://aws.amazon.com/ec2/instance-types)
- The name of the EC2 key-pair you created for this region

> **NOTE**   It's fine to do a t2.micro while you're playing around with these stacks. But when you deploy your application from chapter 7, you'll need at least t2.small nodes for the RAM requirements of Couchbase. You can find pricing information at https://aws.amazon.com/ec2/pricing.

> **NOTE**   If you haven't yet set up your AWS CLI tools, do so now with aws configure. The process is fairly self-explanatory, but you can read the documentation at http://mng.bz/fsfG.

Let's fire it up:

You can check out the stack-creation status and also run the wait command to have the CLI return only when creation is complete:

```
$ aws --output text cloudformation describe-stacks
... CREATE_IN_PROGRESS ...
$ aws cloudformation wait stack-create-complete --stack-name coreosinaction
```

Returns 0 on CREATE_COMPLETE and non-0 if there are any failures

> **NOTE**   If you get stuck or can't make sense of the stack status, you can always log in to the AWS web console and look at the CloudFormation event tab for your stack.

You should be able to query the output object from your CloudFormation stack once the status has reached CREATE_COMPLETE. These outputted configuration items will be useful in chapters 8 and 9:

```
$ aws --output text cloudformation describe-stacks \
  --stack-name coreosinaction \
  --query 'Stacks[0].Outputs[*].[OutputValue]'
```
Query to get the output values

```
coreosinaction-s3backup-1eunpnsppx78f
coreosinaction-LoadBalan-D5IYNEXB783K-2021937736.
us-west-2.elb.amazonaws.com
```
S3 bucket name
ELB host name

Now that your stack is up and running, you can get into your cluster and confirm that everything is set up.

LOGGING IN

First, find the IP of one of your instances so you can log in and check out the cluster. You can do this through the web console, or you can use the AWS CLI. Unfortunately, the EC2 instances aren't considered stack resources, because they're in an ASG, so you have to tack on some filters and queries to get back the IPs:

```
$ aws --output text ec2 describe-instances \        ◁───  Generic describe-all-
  --filter Name=tag:aws:cloudformation:stack-name,Values=coreosinaction \  ◁─┐  instances API request
  --query 'Reservations[*].Instances[0].[PublicIpAddress]'      ◁───┐
54.149.189.24                                    Output query that returns the
54.213.46.236                               PublicIpAddress of each instance found
54.186.111.47
                                                 This filter is sent with the
                                                request to get back a subset.
```

> **NOTE** The AWS CLI tool is powerful. You can read more about its advanced features at http://mng.bz/w17N.

Using the key-pair you specified in the parameters (make sure you've set the appropriate permissions for it as an SSH key, as well), you can log in to one of your cluster nodes:

```
$ ssh \
  -i <path to your key> \        ◁───  Optional if you set up the
  core@54.149.189.24                   key in your SSH config or
...                                    added it to ssh-agent
CoreOS stable (1068.10.0)

...
core@ip-10-1-2-246 ~ $
```

You can do some checks to make sure everything has been set up correctly:

```
core@ip-10-1-2-246 ~ $ fleetctl list-machines      ◁───  Checks the fleet
MACHINE          IP              METADATA                 cluster status
4b3ea058...      10.1.2.246      -
6b113e17...      10.1.3.129      -
ba357666...      10.1.1.253      -                              Checks
                                                               docker0's IP
core@ip-10-1-2-246 ~ $ ip addr show dev docker0 scope global   ◁─┘
3: docker0: <NO-CARRIER,BROADCAST,MULTICAST,UP>          This IP should be in the
    ➥mtu 1500 qdisc noqueue state DOWN group default     subnet you assigned to
      link/ether 02:42:63:ae:aa:30 brd ff:ff:ff:ff:ff:ff flannel in cloud-config in
      inet 10.10.33.1/24 scope global docker0     ◁───   section 8.3.2.
        valid_lft forever preferred_lft forever

core@ip-10-1-2-246 ~ $ df -h /var/lib/docker/      ◁───  Ensures that /var/lib/docker
Filesystem       Size  Used Avail Use% Mounted on        was mounted with your
/dev/xvdb        9.6G  137M  9.5G   2% /var/lib/docker    new 10 GB volume
```

NOTE If you ever need to delete your stack, use `aws cloudformation delete-stack --stackname coreosinaction`. But remember, you can't have duplicate stack names; so, if you want to use `coreosinaction` again, you'll have to wait until it's *completely* deleted, which can take a few minutes.

You now have a production-ready cluster in AWS. Feel free to change parameters around and tune things exactly the way you want them. Add more parameters to reference in your CloudFormation template so you can have different inputs for different deployments: for example, a staging environment with three nodes and a production environment with six. You should be able to create and destroy stacks easily now. The next chapter covers the deployment of your application stack to your new cluster in AWS, as well as how to start automating all your deployments with tools in AWS.

Don't forget to turn off the lights. You may want to destroy your CloudFormation cluster if you don't want to pay for it overnight. You can check your billing dashboard at https://console.aws.amazon.com/billing/home.

8.2 *Summary*

- Be sure to read AWS's documentation on CloudFormation; it's well constructed and contains good examples.
- Pay close attention to dependent objects, which things you can change in CloudFormation with no interruption, and which cause a replacement of the object (resulting in downtime).
- Remember that changes to `cloud-config` require re-creation in order to take effect.
- Keep the results from the OUTPUTS of your stack handy; they represent the critical touch-points for interacting with your system.

Bringing it together: deployment

9

This chapter covers

- Automating your deployment to AWS
- Deploying your application to your AWS infrastructure
- Pushing incremental changes to your application

Your development cluster is set up, your production cluster is set up, and you've architected a full application stack for performance scaling and availability. Now, you have to figure out how you're going to tackle deployment. There are many, many models for constructing deployment mechanics, and many options for continuous integration systems, task schedulers, and build systems. After chapter 8, you have two major systems to rely on: CoreOS and AWS. You want to be able to do something that fits both systems without creating deep dependencies between them.

In this chapter, you'll create a workflow that's pretty generic; it will cut a few corners to remain generic and avoid bringing more components into the system. When you start building this kind of pipeline for your own applications, you'll probably use a variety of other tools, but this example provides the basic inputs of a deployment system that you can plug into your tooling.

Ultimately, this means you're going to create something in AWS that eventually flips a value in etcd, but you want to do it without

- Building out new EC2 VMs to do orchestration
- Running an agent on your CoreOS nodes that only works in AWS

I've established these constraints for a couple of reasons. First, adding infrastructure that becomes a dependency of other infrastructure is a bit of an antipattern for the twelve-factor methodology; it tightly couples two systems. Second, your AWS deployments should be functionally similar to how deployments work in your local Vagrant cluster, to reduce "it works on my machine" syndrome.

Software development in your organization undoubtedly goes through some kind of lifecycle. Services that support the software may go through a similar process. In the process you followed in chapters 6 and 7 to architect your system, the final results were Docker containers and service-unit files. You want to reliably (and with some amount of abstraction) deploy that software and those services into your brand-new production cluster, as rapidly as you did in your local development environment.

In this chapter, you'll add/build some new things:

- A pipeline in AWS to trigger etcd to give the sidekick's context
- A gateway so you can execute that trigger remotely (from Docker Hub webhooks)
- Modified sidekicks to get deployment context from etcd

The big takeaway will be how to deploy software to a CoreOS cluster running in AWS with a single touchpoint that doesn't require you to directly interact with fleet. Figure 9.1 shows what you'll build: you'll use AWS Lambda, AWS API Gateway, and Docker Hub to initiate a sidekick-controlled deploy via etcd.

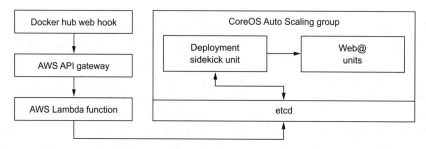

Figure 9.1 Deployment pipeline

9.1 New CloudFormation objects

Yes, you get to add more objects to the ever-growing CloudFormation template!

- An input parameter that serves as a pseudo API deploy key
- An output key that you can drop into Docker Hub's webhook configuration
- A Lambda function that sets a key on your internal etcd load balancer
- An API Gateway configuration to create the endpoint for the webhook

In this chapter, I assume you've completed the previous chapter and understand, for example, that a `Parameter` object goes into the `Parameters` section of the Cloud-Formation file. You'll create the parameter and output objects first, and at the end of the section, you'll run an `update-stack` command.

> **NOTE** If in doubt about your YAML, just like the last chapter, the completed CloudFormation template for this chapter is available in the book's code repository (code/ch9/ch9-cfn-cluster.yml).

9.1.1 Parameter and output

You'll add one new parameter and one new output object. They're related, as you'll see.

Listing 9.1 Parameters

```
DeployKeyPath:          ◁────── For this, you need a randomly
  Description: Long URI component used as a passphrase (in a URI)
  ⇨for deployment. (e.g. pwgen -A 64 1)
  Type: String
  MinLength: 64
  MaxLength: 128
  NoEcho: true
  AllowedPattern: "[a-z0-9]*"
  ConstraintDescription: Must be 64-128 characters
```

For this, you need a randomly generated URL-safe string.

Listing 9.2 Outputs

```
DeployHook:             ◁────── URL you can put into
  Description: URL to put in Docker Hub web hook        Docker Hub webhook
  Value: !Sub "https://${DeployApi}.execute-api.${AWS::Region}
  ⇨.amazonaws.com/prod/${DeployKeyPath}"   ◁─┐ Generates the URL from the
                                              │ objects you'll create shortly
                                              │ and the DeployKeyPath
```

The final product from the modifications of your CloudFormation stack is a URL that causes your CoreOS cluster to update the web application. Unfortunately, the Docker Hub webhook feature doesn't come from a specific IP block and doesn't support custom headers, so you're forced here to make this URL public. The (admittedly less-than-secure) solution is to use the URL like an API key with a reasonable amount of entropy, which would be extremely difficult to guess. Because you're using AWS API Gateway, though, if you wanted to add a more secure trigger—for example, from your CI system—doing so would be trivial.

Here's the worst-case scenario, given the way you're going to construct this. If someone brute-forced—for example, https://<YOUR API GATEWAY>/prod/ iheph6 un2ropiodei7kamo7eegoo2kethai3cohfaicaegae4ea8ahheriedoo1w—and figured out the right payload, the worst they could do would be to cause the service to restart very quickly. When you hook up APIs like this in the real world, security is your responsibility. As mentioned in the introduction to this chapter, this is an interaction you may want to control with another system that's more appropriate to your workflow and security requirements. You'll get started with the `Resources` next.

9.1.2   *AWS Lambda*

AWS Lambda is a newer service in AWS that lets you run snippets of code (Node.js, Python, or Java) in reaction to events in AWS. It has an interesting pricing model: you're charged in units of 100 ms for how long it takes a task to complete. This makes it great for quick, task-oriented operations like asynchronous deployments. You're going to set up the event emitter (AWS API Gateway) in the next subsection, but you'll set up your Lambda function here.

First, you need a new IAM role for Lambda so that it can do things in your VPCs.

```
Listing 9.3   Lambda role

LambdaDeployRole:
  Type: AWS::IAM::Role
  Properties:
    AssumeRolePolicyDocument:
      Version: 2012-10-17
      Statement:
        - Action: "sts:AssumeRole"
          Effect: Allow
          Principal: { Service: lambda.amazonaws.com }
    Path: /
    ManagedPolicyArns:
      - "arn:aws:iam::aws:policy/service-role/AWSLambdaBasicExecutionRole"
      - "arn:aws:iam::aws:policy/service-
    role/AWSLambdaVPCAccessExecutionRole"
```

These policies are provided by AWS, so you don't have to create custom policies as you did for flannel.

Now let's get into the Lambda function. The short script is inlined here, much like cloud-config from chapter 8. Lambda does *not* support inlining Java; for consistency, this example uses Node.js, so you don't have to worry about newlines or whitespace in the `Code` field.

```
Listing 9.4   Lambda function

DeployLambda:
  Type: AWS::Lambda::Function
  DependsOn: [ CoreOSSecurityGroup, LambdaDeployRole ]
```

You want this Lambda function to be able to talk on your CoreOS subnets...

...and you want it in the CoreOS security group.

```yaml
    Properties:
      VpcConfig:
        SubnetIds: [ !Ref SubnetA, !Ref SubnetB, !Ref SubnetC ]
        SecurityGroupIds: [ !Ref CoreOSSecurityGroup ]
      Role: !GetAtt [ LambdaDeployRole, Arn ]
      Timeout: 2
      Handler: index.handler
      Runtime: nodejs4.3
      Code:
        ZipFile: !Sub
          - |
            const options = {
              host: '${host}',
              port: 2379,
              path: '/v2/keys/coreos.com/deploy',
              method: 'PUT',
              headers: {'Content-Type': 'application/x-www-form-urlencoded'}
            };
            exports.handler = (event, context, callback) => {
              if (event['push_data'].tag === 'production') {
                const payload = event.repository.name;
                const req = require('http').request(options);
                req.write(`value=${!payload}`);
                req.end(() => callback(null, `deploy:${!payload}`));
              } else {
                callback(null, 'non-production push');
              }
            };
          - host: !GetAtt [ InternalEtcdLB, DNSName ]
```

Attaches the function to the role you created in listing 9.3

2-second timeout: more than enough for this simple function

Similar to the Base64 function in chapter 8, except that it makes a zip file for Lambda to consume

Sets up the options for the connection, connects to the internal etcd load balancer you created in chapter 8, and targets the /coreos.com/deploy key

Part of Docker Hub's payload contains the container tag. You only want to take actions if that tag is "production".

Sets the Docker repo name as the value for the deploy key

Still emits a success if the tag isn't "production".

Replaces the "${host}" string in the const options object.

There's a little complexity here, but nothing you haven't seen before if you read the code for the sidekick units in previous chapters. The only difference here is that you're interacting with etcd without the help of a handy Node.js library (just the built-in `http` module), and you're hitting the internal etcd load balancer you created in chapter 8 rather than hitting a node directly. You're basically keying the deployment on a particular Docker tag. If that tag is pushed to Docker Hub, this code pushes a new value to an etcd key.

NOTE If you want to read more about the options for Lambda for Cloud-Formation, you can find the documentation at http://mng.bz/57Br.

Finish by giving API Gateway permission to invoke the Lambda function.

Listing 9.5 Lambda permission

```yaml
LambdaPermission:
  Type: AWS::Lambda::Permission
  DependsOn: [ DeployLambda ]
```

```
Properties:
  Action: "lambda:InvokeFunction"
  FunctionName: !GetAtt [ DeployLambda, Arn ]
  Principal: apigateway.amazonaws.com
```

9.1.3 *API Gateway*

API Gateway lets you trigger Lambda functions and pass any HTTP parameters along with them. You'll add only one resource with one method; but it requires a bunch of discrete resources to work, so you have to include a good deal of boilerplate configuration to initiate this resource.

Listing 9.6 Rest API and resource

```
DeployApi:                        ◁────── Base API Gateway resource
  Type: AWS::ApiGateway::RestApi
  Properties: { Name: deploy-coreosinaction }
DeployResource:
  Type: AWS::ApiGateway::Resource
  DependsOn: [ DeployApi ]
  Properties:                                                Reference to the
    ParentId: !GetAtt [ DeployApi, RootResourceId ]  ◁────┤ root (/) resource
    PathPart: !Ref DeployKeyPath   ◁┈┈┐
    RestApiId: !Ref DeployApi            Reference to the
                                         DeployKeyPath input parameter
```

Connects it to the API (arrow to RestApiId line)

The base resource is a lot like the base resource in the web load balancer in chapter 8; it doesn't do much of anything on its own until you attach API Gateway resources, methods, deployments, and stages.

Now, you need to define a POST method for this resource and attach it to the Lambda.

Listing 9.7 POST method

```
DeployPOST:
  Type: AWS::ApiGateway::Method        POST method of
  DependsOn: [ DeployLambda ]          the resource
  Properties:                          that's listening
    HttpMethod: POST              ◁┈┈┐
    AuthorizationType: NONE       ◁──────── Open to the world, as
    Integration:                            explained at the
      PassthroughBehavior: WHEN_NO_MATCH    beginning of this section
      Type: AWS
      IntegrationHttpMethod: POST   ◁────┤ POST that API Gateway
      IntegrationResponses: [ StatusCode: 200 ]  will send to the Lambda
      Uri: !Sub
        - "arn:aws:apigateway:${region}:lambda:path/2015-03-31
          ➥/functions/${arn}/invocations"
        - { arn: !GetAtt [ DeployLambda, Arn ], region: !Ref "AWS::Region" }
    MethodResponses: [ StatusCode: 200 ]
    ResourceId: !Ref DeployResource  ◁────┐
    RestApiId: !Ref DeployApi              │ Attaches to the resource
                                             and API from listing 9.6
```

Assembles the path to the Lambda function (arrow to Uri line)

Next, you construct a "deployment" for API Gateway.

Listing 9.8   Deployment

```
DeployDeployment:
  DependsOn: DeployPOST
  Type: AWS::ApiGateway::Deployment
  Properties: { RestApiId: !Ref DeployApi, StageName: DummyStage }
DeployProdStage:
  Type: AWS::ApiGateway::Stage
  Properties:
    DeploymentId: !Ref DeployDeployment
    MethodSettings: [ { ResourcePath: !Sub "/${DeployKeyPath}",
      ➥HttpMethod: POST } ]
    RestApiId: !Ref DeployApi
    StageName: prod
```

> Initial deployment: uses **DummyStage**, as suggested by the AWS documentation

> **Names the stage deployment "prod"**

> In this stage deployment, you need to reference your methods.

Your API Gateway should be ready to go, and you can move on to updating your stack.

9.1.4   *Updating your stack*

The command to update your stack is similar to the one you used to create it:

```
$ aws cloudformation update-stack \
  --stack-name coreosinaction \
  --template-body file://./code/ch9/ch9-cfn-cluster.yml \
  --capabilities CAPABILITY_IAM \
  --parameters \
  ParameterKey=DeployKeyPath,ParameterValue=ahmup4equa... \
    ParameterKey=InstanceType,UsePreviousValue=true \
    ParameterKey=DiscoveryURL,UsePreviousValue=true \
    ParameterKey=AllowSSHFrom,UsePreviousValue=true \
    ParameterKey=KeyPair,UsePreviousValue=true
```

> **Stack that you already have**

> Path to the updated CloudFormation template

> The rest of the parameters have to be there, but you can set them to use the previous value.

> **New parameter for the deployment URL, 64–128 characters**

Once that's finished, look at the outputs and take note of the generated API Gateway URL:

```
aws --output text cloudformation describe-stacks \
  --stack-name coreosinaction \
  --query 'Stacks[0].Outputs[*].[OutputValue]'

https://zl2hgu19sk.execute-api.us-west-2.amazonaws.com/prod/ahmup4equa...
...
```

> **Truncated here for brevity, but keep this handy**

Test this endpoint:

```
$ curl -X POST -H 'Content-Type: application/json' \
  https://zl2hgu19sk.execute-api.us-west-2.amazonaws.com/prod/ahmup4equa... \
  --data '{"push_data": {"tag": "production"}, "repository":
  ➥{"name": "ch6-web"}}'

"deploy:ch6-web"      ◁———— Success!
```

> Important parts of the Docker Hub payload

What you've built here is essentially a pathway into your CoreOS etcd cluster. You can follow or extend this pattern to build any kind of administrative tooling to interact with your cluster, effectively giving you the ability to build a custom API for specifically managing your services. You can take this further and build more robust authentication and authorization systems into API Gateway, as well as add more interesting functionality to your Lambdas. For example, you could build a Lambda to fire up more compute workers or run a search on your Couchbase or any other data system.

You can finally move on to the initial deployment of your software and test the deployment trigger. The next section will briefly describe the new web sidekick to orchestrate the deployment, and go over pushing out all of your service files.

9.2   *Deploying the app!*

You're ready to get started on the actual deployment of your application. But not so fast: the first thing you have to do is create a new sidekick unit file for the web that can react to etcd events to redeploy your web application. If you apply this pattern to your own applications, you'll have to make deployment sidekicks for any of them that you want to deploy automatically. Let's get this out of the way first, and then move on to deploying the application.

9.2.1   *Web sidekick*

You did a lot of sidekick functionality in chapters 4 and 7. You're adding one more here that you'll attach to the state of the web@ unit template. Like your other sidekicks, this should run on the same machine as the web instance it's bound to. Call the new sidekick web-sidekick@.service.

> **Listing 9.9   code/ch9/webapp/web-sidekick@.service**

```
[Unit]
Description=Web Service Sidekick %i

[Service]
TimeoutStartSec=0          ┐ You want a quick restart
RestartSec=1             ◁─┘ for this sidekick.                      Exits when the
Restart=always                                                      value changes...
ExecStart=/usr/bin/etcdctl watch /coreos.com/deploy       ◁─┘
ExecStop=/usr/bin/docker pull mattbailey/ch6-web:production ◁─┐
ExecStop=/usr/bin/fleetctl stop web@%i.service      ◁─┐      │ ...then pulls the
ExecStop=/usr/bin/fleetctl start web@%i.service           │  │ latest version of the
                                                          │  │ container with the
[X-Fleet]                                                 │  │ "production" tag...
MachineOf=web@%i.service                                  │
                                                          └ ...and restarts
                                                            the web service.
```

Also tweak the web@.service file a little so that you're pulling the `production` tag.

```
[Unit]
Description=Express and Socket.io Web Service %i
Requires=flanneld.service
After=flanneld.service

[Service]
RestartSec=5
Restart=always
ExecStartPre=-/usr/bin/docker rm -f web-%i
ExecStartPre=/usr/bin/docker pull mattbailey/ch6-web:production    ◁─────
ExecStart=/usr/bin/docker run \
  --rm \
  -p 3000:3000 \
  -e NODE_ENV=production \
  --name web-%i \
  mattbailey/ch6-web:production    ◁─────     ...and here.
ExecStop=-/usr/bin/docker rm -f web-%i

[X-Fleet]
Conflicts=web@*.service
```

Change the tag here...

Now you can start up your services in your AWS cluster!

9.2.2 *Initial deployment*

Make sure your local `fleetctl` is set up properly to use your AWS cluster:

```
$ export FLEETCTL_TUNNEL=54.187.209.53        ◁─────
$ fleetctl list-machines
MACHINE      IP           METADATA
1efc44d5...  10.1.3.185   -                   ◁─────
7aa773e3...  10.1.1.57    -
c2a9c9c4...  10.1.2.174   -
```

One of the public IPs you fetched in chapter 8

You should be able to see the machines in your cluster.

Also, set the etcd key for the workers to fetch some Twitter data:

```
$ etcdctl set /config/worker/auth '{ "consumer_key":"Your Consumer Key",
⮕"consumer_secret":"Your Consumer Secret",
⮕"access_token_key":"Your Access Token",
⮕"access_token_secret":"Your Access Token Secret" }'    ◁─┘
```

From chapter 7, section 7.1.2

Now, change directory into where you have all your service units, and spin them all up:

```
$ fleetctl start \
  code/ch9/couchbase@{1..3}.service \
  code/ch9/couchbase-sidekick@{1..3}.service \
  code/ch9/conductor/conductor.service \
  code/ch9/memcached@{1..3}.service \
  code/ch9/memcached-sidekick@{1..3}.service \
  code/ch9/webapp/web@{1..3}.service \
  code/ch9/webapp/web-sidekick@{1..3}.service
```

Keep
checking
list-units
until all
services are
active/running.

```
$ fleetctl list-units
UNIT                            MACHINE                    ACTIVE   SUB
conductor.service               1efc44d5.../10.1.3.185     active   running
couchbase-sidekick@1.service    7aa773e3.../10.1.1.57      active   running
couchbase-sidekick@2.service    1efc44d5.../10.1.3.185     active   running
couchbase-sidekick@3.service    c2a9c9c4.../10.1.2.174     active   running
couchbase@1.service             7aa773e3.../10.1.1.57      active   running
couchbase@2.service             1efc44d5.../10.1.3.185     active   running
couchbase@3.service             c2a9c9c4.../10.1.2.174     active   running
memcached-sidekick@1.service    7aa773e3.../10.1.1.57      active   running
memcached-sidekick@2.service    c2a9c9c4.../10.1.2.174     active   running
memcached-sidekick@3.service    7aa773e3.../10.1.1.57      active   running
memcached@1.service             7aa773e3.../10.1.1.57      active   running
memcached@2.service             c2a9c9c4.../10.1.2.174     active   running
memcached@3.service             7aa773e3.../10.1.1.57      active   running
web-sidekick@1.service          c2a9c9c4.../10.1.2.174     active   running
web-sidekick@2.service          1efc44d5.../10.1.3.185     active   running
web-sidekick@3.service          7aa773e3.../10.1.1.57      active   running
web@1.service                   c2a9c9c4.../10.1.2.174     active   running
web@2.service                   1efc44d5.../10.1.3.185     active   running
web@3.service                   7aa773e3.../10.1.1.57      active   running
```

Next, confirm that your application is up and running by hitting the ELB with `curl`.
You can fetch the ELB hostname with the AWS CLI:

```
$ aws --output text cloudformation describe-stacks \
  --stack-name coreosinaction \                            Gets the stack
  --query 'Stacks[0].Outputs[*]'                           outputs
URL to put in Docker Hub web hook DeployHook
  ➡ https://<YOUR API GATEWAY HOST>
  ➡ /prod/eivi1leecojai3fephievie1ohsuo6sheenga2chaip8oph5doo5bethohg2uv6i
S3 Bucket for Backups Backup  coreosinaction-s3backup-1swvnfetvdowk
ELB Hostname  ELB coreo-LoadB-....us-west-2.elb.amazonaws.com ← ELB hostname

$ curl -I coreo-LoadB-19KFCGFCVRC7M-644524966.us-west-2.elb.amazonaws.com
HTTP/1.1 200 OK                      Should return with Express
X-Powered-By: Express            ◄── as the X-Powered-By
...
```

Also, start up the workers from chapter 7 for a bit—but remember to stop them,
because they'll quickly be rate limited:

```
$ fleetctl start code/ch9/worker/worker@{1..6}.service  ◄── Starts them
...
$ fleetctl destroy code/ch9/worker/worker@{1..6}.service  ◄┐ Destroys them
                                                            │ after a while
```

You can now visit the load balancer in your browser to see the same site you deployed
to your dev environment back in chapter 7. If you visit http://<YOUR ELB>:8091/
index.html, you should be able to access your Couchbase admin panel.

     You should be starting to see the big picture of deploying a complex application
out to your infrastructure in AWS by combining the tools and commands you've

learned in the previous chapters. In the next section, you'll make a change to your web app and test your automated deployment.

9.3 Automated deployment

This section goes over how to use the Lambda hook you set up earlier. Keep handy the URL that came out of the `Outputs` request for your stack in section 9.1.4:

```
URL to put in Docker Hub web hook DeployHook
  ➥https://<YOUR API GATEWAY HOST>
  ➥/prod/eivi1leecojai3fephievie1ohsuo6sheenga2chaip8oph5doo5bethohg2uv6i
```

If you want to follow along with this example, you'll obviously have to use your own Docker Hub account, along with your own published web app.

9.3.1 Docker Hub setup

Go to https://hub.docker.com, and go into the webhook config for your repository. For example, mine is at https://hub.docker.com/r/mattbailey/ch6-web/~/settings/webhooks/ (see figure 9.2). Click the + to add a new hook.

> **NOTE** This example uses Docker Hub primarily because it's an easy pathway to set up and isn't another service you have to construct for this example. Anything could exist in its place: a CI system, task-execution system, GitHub hook, Slack command, and so on.

Figure 9.2 Add a webhook.

Name your webhook, and then paste in the API Gateway URL (see figure 9.3) and click Save.

You're ready to make some modifications to your app and automatically deploy it when it's pushed to Docker Hub. Let's give it a shot.

WEB HOOKS   ✕

Webhook name	Webhook URL
web deploy	https://ywko0m1xa9.execute-api.us-west-2.an

Cancel   Save

Figure 9.3   Save the webhook.

9.3.2   *Pushing a change*

Let's make a simple style change so it's obvious what you've done. In the index.html file, add the following new line after the `<script>` tag for socket.io:

```
<script src="/socket.io/socket.io.js"></script>          ◁──── Existing line
<style>body { background-color: #000; color: #fff; }</style>  ◁──── Add this line.
```

Save the file, and build and run your Docker image. Then, push it to Docker Hub, using the `production` tag:

```
$ docker build -t mattbailey/ch6-web:production .        ◁─┐ Make sure you tag it with
Sending build context to Docker daemon 14.34 kB            │ "production" here...
Step 1 : FROM library/node:onbuild
...
$ docker push mattbailey/ch6-web:production              ◁──── ...and in the push.
The push refers to a repository [docker.io/mattbailey/ch6-youb]
...
```

The rest should be automatic. Go back to your website and reload a few times; after maybe a minute, your site should appear with white text on a black background. Congratulations! You've set up an automated deployment pipeline.

You can easily integrate this kind of workflow into the common continuous-integration or source-control hooks you normally use. For example, perhaps you have CircleCI or Jenkins do the Docker build on a push to a GitHub repo branch and then push it out to Docker Hub to trigger this deploy. Now, instead of manually destroying and re-creating services with `fleetctl` to deploy a new version, you're more or less hands-off your CoreOS cluster after the initial deployment, until you want to remove or add new services. This is the point at which your CoreOS system becomes more self-service for developers; you can continue to add automation around CoreOS to remove a lot of human error related to running robust services.

The final chapter looks at the long-term maintenance of this deployment, how to tune the infrastructure for scale, and what's on the horizon for CoreOS.

9.4 *Summary*

- Use AWS's features to automate as much as you can in your CoreOS cluster.
- Beware of tightly coupling AWS systems: note that you didn't make your Lambda function directly interact with fleet.
- Make sure you use etcd as an abstraction point of loose coupling: for example, you should be able to trigger any automation from `curl` to etcd.
- Don't forget to consider security and authorization restraints in your real-world pipelines.
- Tune your stack outputs. CloudFormation can provide a lot of useful information to help with automation.
- The final step to close the loop for *your* implementation is to integrate your CI tools and source-control system.

System administration

10

This chapter covers

- Logging and maintaining backups in your stack
- Horizontally scaling your cluster
- An introduction to rk

You've come a long way in your journey with CoreOS: from the basics of understanding the OS to building an application and all the related components and deploying it into a production AWS environment. This final chapter goes over what's involved in continued administration of a CoreOS cluster, enhancements and tunables of the environment you built in chapters 8 and 9, and what the future of CoreOS holds.

By the end of this chapter, you should have some clarity about general system administration tasks and workflows: how to consume logs from CoreOS in AWS, how to deal with scaling your existing CoreOS cluster, and backing up persistent data from your Couchbase install and etcd. I'll also touch on how to create services using rkt and give you some details about upcoming projects from CoreOS, like Torus and Clair.

10.1 Logging and backups

Logs (obviously) are among the most basic sets of information for systems administrators. AWS has a log-concentration service built in: CloudWatch Logs. Conveniently, Docker supports this out of the box (along with a lot of other log drivers; see http://mng.bz/m3R3). There are a couple places you can define this configuration: either globally when you start dockerd (which means changing cloud-config) or at the docker run runtime (which means changing your unit file). This section covers both (and you can use both options at the same time), but first you'll have to make some small changes to your AWS environment.

> **NOTE** Again, it's best to use the code repository when you run this stack (code/ch10/ch10-cfn-cluster.yml).

If you want to make this change in your cloud-config, remember that doing so will cause an update to your launch configuration, which will trigger a replacement of all your nodes—meaning you should generate a new discovery token. If you opt to do it in your unit files, you won't have to go through this step, but your unit files will become a little less generic. If you update with the provided S3 linked template, it *does* include the launch-configuration change.

10.1.1 Setting up logs

First, you'll have to add a single resource to your CloudFormation stack. Anywhere in the Resources object, add a CloudWatch LogGroup.

Listing 10.1 LogGroup

```
LogGroup:
  Type: AWS::Logs::LogGroup
  Properties: { RetentionInDays: 7 }
```
As the key implies, this sets how long (in days) CloudWatch will retain log entries.

> **NOTE** Only certain values are valid in the RetentionInDays field. You can read more at http://mng.bz/kQ2T.

It's also useful to add an output to reference this LogGroup so you can easily use the CLI tools to check your logs. Place this in your Outputs object.

Listing 10.2 Output

```
LogGroup:
  Description: CoreOS Log Group Name
  Value: !Ref LogGroup
```
Simple output of the generated LogGroup name

Now that you have a LogGroup with some friendly outputs, you also need to modify the IAM role for your instances so you can write to these logs with the AWS API. In section 8.2.3, you set up the IAM policy for your instances; next, add a few more log permissions.

Listing 10.3   IAM permissions for logs

```
Action:
  - "ec2:CreateRoute"
  - "ec2:DeleteRoute"
  - "ec2:ReplaceRoute"
  - "ec2:ModifyNetworkInterfaceAttribute"
  - "ec2:ModifyInstanceAttribute"
  - "logs:CreateLogStream"
  - "logs:PutLogEvents"
```

Original set of actions from chapter 8

Two new permissions to grant to your instances

If you choose to do your log configuration in your unit files, these are the only changes you have to make; you can go ahead and run your template update with the CLI commands you learned in chapter 9 or via the web console. If you want to make the changes global to the dockerd running in the cluster, continue to the next subsection.

10.1.2   *Updating cloud-config*

Much as you did with flannel, you need to create a drop-in unit for Docker to enable this logging functionality in cloud-config. In section 8.3, you set up user data in the !Sub | user-data document in the Auto Scaling launch configuration. Add the following anywhere under units:.

Listing 10.4   Docker drop-in for `awslogs`

```
- name: docker.service
  drop-ins:
    - name: 10-awslogs.conf
      content: |
        [Service]
        Environment="DOCKER_OPTS=--log-driver=awslogs
        --log-opt awslogs-region=${AWS::Region}
        --log-opt awslogs-group=${LogGroup}"
```

Adds a drop-in to override some settings for the dockerd runtime

Sets a DOCKER_OPTS environment variable to use the awslogs driver for logs

Tells the driver which AWS region you're in, as well as the LogGroup you created in the last subsection

Now, you can go ahead and update your stack and generate a new token at the same time:

```
$ aws cloudformation update-stack \
  --stack-name coreosinaction \
  --template-body file://./code/ch10/ch10-cfn-cluster.yml \
  --capabilities CAPABILITY_IAM \
  --parameters \
    ParameterKey=DeployKeyPath,UsePreviousValue=true \
    ParameterKey=InstanceType,UsePreviousValue=true \
    ParameterKey=DiscoveryURL,ParameterValue=
    $(curl https://discovery.etcd.io/new) \
    ParameterKey=AllowSSHFrom,UsePreviousValue=true \
    ParameterKey=KeyPair,UsePreviousValue=true
```

Path to the updated template for this chapter

Creates a new discovery token

Remember that, if you do this, you'll need to reinitialize your application to apply the change. *All your data will be lost.*

That's all you need for a global setup. Once you start your service again, it should begin emitting logs into CloudWatch. The downside of this global method is that the log streams are named after the Docker container ID, which isn't very informative. Doing this globally is usually in addition to defining the log configuration in service units as a catch-all. Before you view your log events, let's look at what it takes to put the configuration in your units.

10.1.3 awslogs in units

This process is more or less the same as with the main docker.service drop-in; you're adding some flags to the runtime of your service units. Before you do that, get the LogGroup name from the CloudFormation outputs:

```
OUTPUTS CoreOS Log Group Name    LogGroup
    coreosinaction-LogGroup-4OOCJWKBHIWP  ◁─── LogGroup name to capture
```

Now that you have that name, you can put it in your unit files; for the sake of a quick example, you'll use the Hello World example from chapter 3 (code/ch10/helloworld@.service).

Listing 10.5 `awslogs` logs in units

```
[Unit]
Description=Helloworld Service %i
Requires=flanneld.service
After=flanneld.service

[Service]                                         You'll use the simple
RestartSec=5                                       example from this
Restart=always                                     chapter to show logging.
ExecStartPre=-/usr/bin/docker rm -f helloworld-%i
ExecStartPre=/usr/bin/docker pull mattbailey/ch6-helloworld:latest  ◁
ExecStart=/usr/bin/docker run \
    --log-driver=awslogs \
    --log-opt awslogs-region=us-west-2 \
    --log-opt awslogs-group=coreosinaction-LogGroup-4OOCJWKBHIWP \   ◁
    --log-opt awslogs-stream=%m-helloworld-%i \   ◁
    --rm \
    -p 3000:3000 \
    --name helloworld-%i \
    mattbailey/helloworld:latest
ExecStop=-/usr/bin/docker rm -f helloworld-%i

[X-Fleet]
Conflicts=helloworld@*.service                    Names the log stream
                                                  in the log group
```

Selects the appropriate region

Tells Docker to use the awslogs driver,   Drops in the LogGroup name
same as with the dockerd config   from the previous snippet

Start this service with `fleetctl start helloworld@{1..3}.service` as usual. The big difference is the `awslogs-stream` option you add here. This lets you add a much friendlier name to the log stream, so you can more easily identify the source of the logs you're looking at. You haven't used the `%m` template variable before: it resolves to the machine name in the CoreOS cluster, so you can identify which machine the service is running on just by looking at the AWS CloudWatch logs. `%i` is the service instance, as usual.

> **NOTE** You might be tempted to do something like `awslogs-stream=helloworld` and have all services then dump into the same stream. But AWS strongly discourages doing this, due to the way the log-sequence API works. You also don't gain anything, because you can search and view logs across multiple streams in the same `LogGroup`.

10.1.4 Viewing logs

Now that you've got your services configured one way or another to output to Cloud-Watch logs, it's time to view the logs you're streaming to. If you'd like, you can do this using the AWS console and the friendly web UI (https://console.aws.amazon.com/cloudwatch/home), or use the CLI tools to dump some logs:

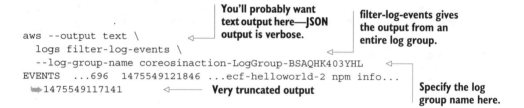

In `text` output mode, you'll see a number of fields: the first is a type designator; `EVENTS` is a log event; `SEARCHEDLOGSTREAMS` tells you which streams in your group were searched; and `NEXTTOKEN` is a way to paginate output. The rest of the fields in the `EVENTS` type are `eventId` (a unique key), `ingestionTime` (epoch time when Cloud-Watch got the event), `logStreamName`, the actual `message`, and finally the emitted epoch `timestamp`.

I recommend looking through the documentation for `aws logs` to learn how to search and get the most out of your logging. Logging with CloudWatch is a convenient option, but you may have other log-aggregation systems in your infrastructure already, likely with richer feature sets.

Now that you've configured a simple log-aggregation service, we'll move on to backups for your persistent data.

> ## A note on monitoring
> Logs provide the most context for useful monitoring in a lot of ways. Setting up queries for your CloudWatch logs to send alerts on some result sets is more suited for an AWS book but is certainly within AWS's feature set. This also goes for monitoring system resources: CPU/RAM/disk usage are all relative to the hosting provider; CoreOS doesn't offer specific tools, although some new projects in the wild support etcd for monitoring discovery (for example, Prometheus: https://prometheus.io).

10.1.5 Backing up data

In chapter 8, you created an S3 bucket and a policy to go with it, in order to have a place to back up your data. You now have some (presumably) important data in your Couchbase cluster that you want to make sure you push into S3 on a regular basis. The process would be similar for any database you're using, with whatever backup tool it ships with. Because you've done a lot of due diligence about setting appropriate keys in etcd, the process becomes fairly simple. This section also demonstrates how to back up the etcd cluster and store it in the S3 bucket.

Before you get started, make sure you note the name of your S3 bucket, either in the AWS web console or from the command-line output of the following command:

```
aws --output text cloudformation describe-stacks
    ⮕--stack-name coreosinaction | grep Backup
OUTPUTS S3 Bucket for Backups Backup
    ⮕coreosinaction-s3backup-1xu0sff666ebx          ⟵─┐ You'll use this bucket
                                                         for backup.
```

Now, let's look at the units for backup. You'll start with Couchbase: as your data store of valuable business information, this is probably the most important thing you have to back up. Other than from etcd (which you'll also back up), Couchbase data is the only thing in your system that isn't ephemeral. Your first backup service should look something like the following listing (code/ch10/couchbase-backup.service).

Listing 10.6 Couchbase backup service

```
[Unit]
Description=Couchbase Backup

[Service]
TimeoutStartSec=0
RestartSec=3600        ⟵─┐ Waits an hour (3,600
Restart=always              seconds) to restart
                       ⟵── Restarts, even on success
ExecStartPre=-/usr/bin/rm -rf /tmp/backup    ⟵─┐
ExecStartPre=/usr/bin/mkdir /tmp/backup         Cleans and creates a
ExecStart=/bin/sh -c ' \                         new backup directory
    docker run --rm \
      -v /tmp/backup:/tmp/backup \      Uses the same image you used
      couchbase:community-4.0.0 \   ⟵── for your Couchbase deployment
```

Uses the first result in the cluster config you stored in etcd

```
cbbackup http://$(etcdctl get `etcdctl ls /services/couchbase/ |
 head -n1`):8091 \
 /tmp/backup \
 -u Administrator -p $(etcdctl get /config/couchbase/password) && \
docker run --rm \
 -v /tmp/backup:/tmp/backup \
 samepagelabs/s3cmd \
 --region=us-west-2 sync /tmp/backup s3://<INSERT_S3_BUCKET_NAME>/'
```

Inserts the S3 bucket name you got from the output of the AWS CLI command

You do several things here. This new unit is meant to restart when it's finished and wait 3,600 seconds every time. You can set this to a smaller interval for testing if you want. You do two Docker runs in this service and remove them (--rm) when they exit, and they both mount the /tmp/backup directory you make. First the backup tool cbbackup runs, and then you use a public image with s3cmd installed to sync the files to S3.

You don't need this to run on any particular node, and you only need it to run on one. So, as you should be used to by now, issue fleetctl start backup.service, and you should be good to go with interval backups of your Couchbase data.

NOTE Couchbase's cbbackup tool automatically creates directories with dates in their names. If you're using some other database, be sure you're manually creating that structure if the tool doesn't do it for you. Alternatively, looking into advanced features of S3, such as versioning, might be useful.

You'll do roughly the same thing with etcd in listing 10.7 (code/ch10/etcd-backup.service). You aren't storing a lot of important stuff in etcd right now, but as a canonical source of configuration in your system, it's useful to be able to back this up. As your application grows and you have to add more configuration around it, this data will become increasingly critical. This backup task is a little easier, because you don't need to use Docker to perform the etcd backup. You do, however, need to make sure you're creating incremental backups, because the etcdctl tool won't create named directories for you.

Listing 10.7 etcd backup service

```
[Unit]
Description=etcd Backup

[Service]
TimeoutStartSec=0
RestartSec=3600
Restart=always
ExecStartPre=-/usr/bin/rm -rf /tmp/etcdbackup
ExecStartPre=-/usr/bin/mkdir /tmp/etcdbackup
ExecStart=/bin/sh -c ' \
  etcdctl backup --backup-dir /tmp/etcdbackup/`date +%%s` --data-dir
 /var/lib/etcd2 && \
  docker run --rm \
```

Dumps the backup into a directory with the epoch time as its name

```
    -v /tmp/etcdbackup:/tmp/etcdbackup \
    samepagelabs/s3cmd \
      --region=us-west-2 sync /tmp/etcdbackup
➥ s3://<INSERT_S3_BUCKET_NAME>/'          ⊲─── Uses the same s3cmd image
```

This effectively does the same thing as the previous service, but for etcd. You can start it as usual with `fleetctl start etcd-backup.service`.

You're now set for backups of your cluster and application stack for this book's example. Obviously, your backup needs for real applications will likely be more complex than the simple cases here, but this is a pattern you should be able to use for any data system. Sometimes, backup operations are fairly expensive to execute, and you may eventually need to delegate those services to a different machine. The next section talks about how to scale out your CoreOS cluster to add capacity for your services.

10.2 Scaling systems

The last part of the equation for a complete system is how to scale your system horizontally. Let's look at these resource dimensions:

- Storage capacity
- Memory
- CPU
- Storage I/O
- Network capacity

These limits are a function of your application stack's performance characteristics, and you'll have to test your application to figure out which ones you'll hit. Storage capacity is usually something you can predict, and although you might want to scale out horizontally for that, it might be worth considering logically splitting a cluster between storage and compute. Memory usage is *usually* predictable, and you might not need to monitor it for scale unless you're running something like Elasticsearch or Redis Cluster. Realistically, you're unlikely to hit limits on network capacity or storage I/O without also spiking the CPU pretty high, so CPU is a good metric to initially be the driving force for scaling.

You'll start this section by making some small modifications to your CloudFormation template to allow you to easily add capacity. Then, we'll move on to discuss how to partition scaling in the cluster.

10.2.1 Scaling your cluster

CoreOS provides a simple way to horizontally scale out a cluster of machines. Removing a machine is a little more difficult with etcd2, because it will no longer automatically eject a machine as version 1 did. To change your scale, you have to make some minimal changes. First, you have to modify your CloudFormation template. You'll parameterize this so you can adjust it more easily in the future. In the `Parameters` section of the CloudFormation cluster, add the following.

Listing 10.8   Manual scaling with a parameter

```
DesiredCapacity:
  Description: Desired nodes in the CoreOS Cluster
  Type: Number
  Default: 3
  MinValue: 3
```

This should be self-explanatory at this point. You add a new parameter value so you can change the desired capacity more easily.

Next, you need to reference that parameter in your Auto Scaling group ASG. Find the `CoreOSServerAutoScale` resource in your template, and change the `Desired-Capacity` property as shown next.

Listing 10.9   Desired capacity from the parameter

```
CoreOSServerAutoScale:
  ...
  Properties:
    DesiredCapacity: !Ref DesiredCapacity   ⟵──┐   If you've been following along
  ...                                           │   exactly, this will be set to 3
                                                │   before you change it.
```

Now, you can update your CloudFormation stack. Use the `update-stack` command from section 10.1.2, and add the new parameter: `ParameterKey=DesiredCapacity,` `ParameterValue=4`. You should see a new node in your ASG, and a new CoreOS node should eventually appear in your cluster if you run the usual `fleetctl list-machines`.

You have a new node in your cluster, but nothing is running on it. There are a few ways you can get your services running. Either you can add a new instance of any service (such as `fleetctl start helloworld@4.service`), or you can change your service into a global one. Usually, you leave out the template designation for this service—for example, helloworld@.service would become helloworld.service—and add the following lines:

```
...
[X-Fleet]
Global=true
```

Now, when you `fleetctl start helloworld.service`, it will ensure that the service is running on every available machine.

Your services are up on the larger cluster. Next, you need a way to *remove* an instance from the cluster. This is a little hairier. etcd won't automatically remove a machine from a cluster if it stops responding. This is mostly a good thing: you don't want a node completely removed if it's rebooting or has become unresponsive. To scale *down*, you need to check out the cluster's health and then issue the `etcdctl` command to remove a node. You can do this in a quick script:

```
$ etcdctl cluster-health | \
  grep unreachable | \
  cut -d' ' -f2 | \
  xargs etcdctl member remove
```

This checks the cluster health and removes unreachable members by their machine name. CoreOS is designed to be a complete platform, so the pattern for scaling down a cluster isn't as clean as adding new nodes. The intention is that you have a pool of capacity in your CoreOS cluster, and you're typically scaling various services within it. You add nodes to that pool as you outgrow it; but in most cases, you're not likely to want to remove resources.

Next, let's look at how you can partition for scaling.

10.2.2 Scale partitioning

Now that you know how to scale up and down in your clusters, we can discuss the various ways in which you might want to break up a cluster into logical groups for scaling. Fleet has the ability to assign metadata to clusters that can help with this partitioning. You'll probably want to keep one cluster for etcd so that your configuration remains consistent; but you may want to run, say, your Couchbase cluster on nodes with more CPUs and larger disks.

By partitioning your cluster into different logical groups with different scaling goals, you can maintain a cluster that's more flexible for your needs and that consists of a heterogeneous mix of machines. ASGs in AWS have a fixed instance type, so in order to do this, you have to write a new group resource in your CloudFormation stack. For the sake of brevity, I won't paste the entire second ASG into the book, but you can find it in the CloudFormation template mentioned at the beginning of this chapter.

In short, you'll add a new launch configuration called `DatabaseCoreOSServer-LaunchConfig` and a new ASG called `DatabaseCoreOSServerAutoScale`. The launch configuration has a small part added to its cloud-config in `UserData`:

```
#cloud-config                         Already present
coreos:
  fleet:
    metadata: "role=database"         Adds metadata to fleet for this partition
...
```

This is just a snippet from `UserData` to illustrate how you'd add metadata for fleet (`role=database`). If you haven't already done so, you can update your stack with the linked template. You should have a total of seven nodes in your cluster: four from the last section, where you added a new node to the three-node cluster, and three from this new ASG.

Now that you have a couple of partitions set up, you can make sure your database services are running in the right place.

10.2.3 *Migrating services*

One feature of fleet's extensions to systemd is that you can ensure that some services run (or don't run) on certain machines based on a number of parameters. One we haven't looked into yet is the metadata parameter. You have a logical partition of your cluster with the fleet metadata role set to database, so you can tune your Couchbase unit files to make sure they're running on the correct machines.

First, check your cluster to ensure that you have all the nodes and metadata is properly set:

```
MACHINE          IP          METADATA
2e3ebbb2...      10.1.3.177      role=database
32616658...      10.1.3.21       -
540cfa08...      10.1.2.176      -
6db82152...      10.1.1.111      -
b0b00cea...      10.1.2.122      role=database
d684931b...      10.1.1.224      role=database
f1c9bf2f...      10.1.1.75       -
```

As you can see, three nodes have role=database in their metadata. To key on this, change the couchbase@.service template by adding the following line at the end:

```
...
[X-Fleet]
Conflicts=couchbase@*
MachineMetadata=role=database        ◁──  The only line you add
```

Now, you can migrate your Couchbase cluster over to the new machines in this role. Because you designed this system to tolerate Couchbase nodes failing and moving around, if you destroy and create new services one at a time, you should be able to move the entire cluster without losing any data. You'll have to make sure you watch the output of the conductor as you're doing this, to keep track of the data balancing across the cluster. In a separate terminal, you can follow the conductor's log with fleetctl:

You should see this when   **This will take some time,**
you remove a node.   **as it did in chapter 9.**

```
       $ fleetctl journal -f conductor.service
  └─▷   ... docker[1665]: FIRST_NODE lost, re-setting to: 10.10.81.2
       ... docker[1665]: INFO: rebalancing                    ◁───────────────
  ┌─▷   ... docker[1665]: SUCCESS: rebalanced cluster
       ... docker[1665]: Node added, rebalancing: SUCCESS: server-add 10.10.64.2:8091
       ... docker[1665]: SUCCESS: rebalanced cluster  ◁───┐              △
                                                          │              │
```

Wait for success before you   **Wait for this rebalance before**   **You'll see this when you**
launch another node.   **you destroy another node.**   **launch a new node.**

> **NOTE** If the IP addresses are confusing, remember that you're using flannel, so they're not the same as the IPs reported by fleetctl list-machines.

One by one, issue `fleetctl destroy couchbase@1.service` (wait for rebalance) and `fleetctl start couchbase@1.service` (wait for rebalance). Once this is finished, all of your Couchbase services should be running only on the new nodes you designated for that purpose. For the sake of simplicity in this book, the resource characteristics of this partition are identical to the original cluster; but this illustrates how you could easily change just a part of your cluster to be larger AWS instances or have more storage.

10.3 CoreOS horizon

CoreOS is a rapidly evolving platform. During the writing of this book, new products have been created in the CoreOS family, and more experimental features have stabilized. Take all this at a pace you can handle: it's easy to get overwhelmed by the world of DevOps tooling. This section begins with an overview of some newer functionality and products, and finishes with a deeper dive into rkt, the CoreOS team's new container runtime.

10.3.1 New toys

As of this writing, etcd version 3 has been in an experimental state for a while. It hasn't hit the CoreOS alpha build channel yet, but it's under heavy development. Improvements will include a new way to do TTLs with *leases* that can tie many keys to a single expiration event, big performance increases from using gRPC over HTTP/2, and using gRPC for watchers that don't have to rely on polling. Coupled with changes to data models and improved reliability and concurrency, version 3 should scale out to some truly massive deployments.

On the configuration side, cloud-config is slowly being replaced with a new system called *Ignition* (https://coreos.com/ignition). Most of the CoreOS documentation now shows Ignition configuration (in JSON) next to the equivalent cloud-config YAML. It mostly serves the same purpose; as described by the documentation, Ignition "only runs once and Ignition doesn't handle variable substitution." Amusingly, a week before I started this chapter, AWS CloudFormation began to support YAML as templates and adding more robust variable substitution.

For readers who are security engineers, CoreOS has also released *Clair*: a vulnerability scanner for appc (rkt) and Docker containers (https://coreos.com/clair). It's a full-stack application running on a PostgreSQL database that reads the CVE database, checks images, and sends notifications about issues it finds. Dex (https://github.com/coreos/dex) is also something the security-minded may be interested in as an identity-management system using the OIDC standard. Unfortunately, it doesn't yet include a built-in identity provider (IdP), although that's planned.

The last new product worth discussing is Torus (https://github.com/coreos/torus). Torus solves the same problem that Ceph does: it provides a distributed filesystem with some level of fault tolerance. It shows a lot of promise, but at the time of writing, it's still advertised as being experimental and not suitable for production. It didn't even exist when I was writing the sections of this book that discuss Ceph.

10.3.2 *rkt*

To wrap up this book, we'll dive into rkt: a new container runtime developed by CoreOS to run the arguably more "standardized" Application Container Image (ACI) format. This appears at the end of the book because it's not likely to be part of your workflow any time soon. I'm including it for a couple of reasons: First, it represents a significant development effort by the CoreOS team, and I don't think this book would be complete without at least showing its functionality. Second, while I've been wrapping up these last few chapters, the community around Docker has become a little contentious, and people are starting to look at alternatives—so you may see rkt sooner rather than later. Everything in this section will be done with your Vagrant cluster, rather than your AWS cluster, because rkt is somewhat experimental and the toolchain requires complexity on the workstation side.

The biggest difference between rkt and Docker is that it has no controlling daemon as the parent process of all the containers you run with it. Rather than issue commands to a daemon, when you run a service with rocket, it spawns a new rkt process and your application as its only child or children. When your application exits, that rkt process exits as well (with an exit code of its child). In practice, this means you don't have to rely on a daemon as a single point of failure or major security vector, and also that your init system becomes the parent that directly controls your application state, which takes out a lot of boilerplate configuration and simplifies the architecture from the standpoint of a distributed scheduler (see figure 10.1). If you're familiar with some older process-isolation systems like chroot jails, FreeBSD jail, or Solaris zones, this implementation of containers will seem similar, but with the added benefits of image layering and simple-to-use tooling.

Figure 10.1 is similar to the diagram on the coreos.com page on rkt, but I want to point out a few things. First, regardless of implementation, fleet controls what systemd is doing and can understand the state of the system from context it gathers from systemd. What fleet can't do (without you adding some kind of programmatic callback in a sidekick, for example) is understand the context of how the dockerd daemon is

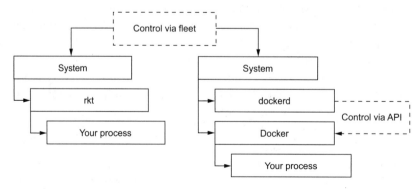

Figure 10.1   rkt vs. Docker process model

interacting with the Docker container process. I've seen rkt described as a way to make containerization boring, and that's essentially what it's doing by not adding a new layer of opaque context.

The other facet of rkt is security by way of signing certificates with GNU Privacy Guard (GPG). This provides an extra layer of certainty that the image you're using is the one you intended, in addition to SSL certificate validation. rkt and ACI are intended as a suite of tools rather than a monolithic tool. If you're going to use rkt in production, and you aren't going to convert Docker images to ACIs, the most important tools to know are ones to help you build rkt images. In this section, we'll go through a part of the Hello World application with Docker from chapter 3 and turn it into an ACI so it can be run with rkt.

Much like Docker, rkt and the appc user-land tools it depends on (such as `acbuild`) run directly only on Linux. This means you'll need to use virtualization for this with Vagrant if you're not using Linux natively. If you skipped any part of the Vagrant setup in chapter 2, make sure you have it set up to deal with building ACIs.

Before we get started, a note on the scope of this section. Much like with Docker, there's a "free if you want your project to be public, monthly cost if you want a private image" service at https://quay.io from which ACIs are served. But a part is missing: you can't (currently) push an ACI that you create into quay.io. You *can* put a Docker project into quay.io, and it will both serve up a Docker repository *and* convert and serve up an ACI at the same time. So, if you want to, you can place your existing containers there and not ever have to create an ACI by yourself, but still use your existing Docker workflow as if they were ACIs.

Unlike with Docker, you don't need an API service to serve custom ACIs. All you need is something to serve flat files over HTTPS; you can read more about it at http://mng.bz/ma8X. This makes setting up your own "registry" for AMIs fairly simple; you can even drop them on AWS S3 following that guide. I won't cover all of that hosting here, but I'll discuss how to build an ACI.

STEP 1: GETTING THE RKT TOOLS RUNNING

First, check out the rkt Git repository from GitHub; for simplicity, I assume you're using `git` via CLI. I also assume you're cloning this repo in the same directory where you have your `helloworld` project directory from chapter 3:

```
$ git clone https://github.com/coreos/rkt.git
...
$ ls
helloworld rkt  # This directory has both helloworld and rkt
$ cd rkt
```

You should now be in the rkt directory. Make the following small edit to the Vagrant-file so you can link the `helloworld` project into the Vagrant machine.

Listing 10.10   Edited Vagrantfile

```
Vagrant.configure('2') do |config|
    # grab Ubuntu 15.10 official image
    config.vm.box = "ubuntu/wily64" # Ubuntu 15.10

    # fix issues with slow DNS http://serverfault.com/a/595010
    config.vm.provider :virtualbox do |vb, override|
        vb.customize ["modifyvm", :id, "--natdnshostresolver1", "on"]
        vb.customize ["modifyvm", :id, "--natdnsproxy1", "on"]
        # add more ram, the default isn't enough for the build
        vb.customize ["modifyvm", :id, "--memory", "1024"]
    end

    config.vm.provider :libvirt do |libvirt, override|
        libvirt.memory = 1024
    end

    config.vm.synced_folder ".", "/vagrant", type: "rsync"
    config.vm.synced_folder "../helloworld", "/app", type: "virtualbox"
    config.vm.provision :shell,
  ➥:privileged => true, :path => "scripts/install-vagrant.sh"
end
```

> The line you add. If you kept the helloworld app somewhere other than in the parent directory, specify that path here.

All you've done so far is add a synced folder to your Vagrant machine config so that you can use the rkt and app container tools for the helloworld project. Fire up the Vagrant machine with vagrant up.

STEP 2: BUILDING YOUR APPLICATION WITH ACBUILD

Now that you're set up with rkt, you can build your app container. Start with the build script, which is similar in concept to a Dockerfile. Edit this file before you ssh into the Vagrant machine.

Listing 10.11   /helloworld/appc-build.sh

> Just like tags in Docker, set the name of your ACI to the hostname where it will eventually be hosted.

> This means you'll be using the Alpine Linux base image from CoreOS on Quay, a minimal distribution.

```
acbuild begin
acbuild set-name mdb.io/helloworld
acbuild dependency add quay.io/coreos/alpine-sh
acbuild run -- apk add nodejs --update-cache --repository
  ➥http://nl.alpinelinux.org/alpine/edge/main
acbuild copy /app /app
acbuild run -- /bin/sh -c "cd /app; npm install"
acbuild set-exec -- /bin/sh -c "cd /app; node app.js"
acbuild port add www tcp 3000
acbuild label add version 0.0.1
acbuild label add arch amd64
acbuild label add os linux
acbuild write helloworld-0.0.1-linux-amd64.aci
acbuild end
```

> You're not using the node:onbuild image, so make sure your dependencies are installed.

> Entry point for the ACI

> Configures ports that this container will use, much like PORT in Docker

> Recommended ACI naming convention

> Various types of metadata are supported; see the acbuild documentation for more examples.

Next, ssh into your Vagrant box and build your ACI with this script:

**Makes sure the project
was synced properly**

**You need to install this additional
component in order for "acbuild
run" lines to run correctly.**

```
$ vagrant ssh
vagrant@vagrant-ubuntu-wily-64:~$ ls /app
appc-build.sh  app.js  Dockerfile  helloworld@.service
   ➥helloworld-sidekick@.service  package.json
vagrant@vagrant-ubuntu-wily-64:~$ sudo apt-get install systemd-container
...
vagrant@vagrant-ubuntu-wily-64:~$ sudo sh /app/appc-build.sh
Downloading quay.io/coreos/alpine-sh: [===============] 2.65 MB/2.65 MB
...
vagrant@vagrant-ubuntu-wily-64:~$ ls -lh *.aci
-rw-r--r-- 1 root root 22M May 26 03:56 helloworld-0.0.1-linux-amd64.aci
```

**Runs your build script, always
with sudo for this build VM**

**Only 22 MB. The ACI
has been created.**

Because the base image here is Alpine Linux (a *very* slim distribution), and because you're not adding a lot of things that might be required by node packages (but not for this helloworld app), the container image weighs in at only 22 MB. Now you can run it with rkt!

STEP 3: RUNNING THE ACI WITH RKT

While still sshed into your Vagrant box, issue the following commands to run and test the ACI:

**Required because you didn't generate
GPG signatures for this image**

**Named port you defined
in appc-build.sh**

**You can fork the
command to a subshell
into the background if
you want to, using &, or
open a new "vagrant
ssh" session to test.**

```
vagrant@vagrant-ubuntu-wily-64:~$ sudo rkt run \
             --insecure-options=image \
             --port=www:3000 \
             helloworld-0.0.1-linux-amd64.aci &
[1] 6917
image: using image from file /usr/lib/rkt/stage1-images/stage1-coreos.aci
image: using image from file /usr/local/bin/stage1-coreos.aci
image: using image from file helloworld-0.0.1-linux-amd64.aci
image: using image from local store for image name quay.io/coreos/alpine-sh
networking: loading networks from /etc/rkt/net.d
networking: loading network default with type ptp
vagrant@vagrant-ubuntu-wily-64:~$ curl 10.0.3.1:3000
hello world
vagrant@vagrant-ubuntu-wily-64:~$ sudo kill -SIGKILL 6917
```

It works!

**Kills the rkt
process**

**Take note of the PID so you can
kill it later, if you forked.**

**Unless you've changed some settings in
VirtualBox, this should be the IP. If it's not,
check for "ip addr show lxcbr0".**

You've built and run your first ACI. As you've learned, how you get your ACIs to your infrastructure is an open question, but with some simple proposed solutions. Serving up files over HTTP in production is beyond the scope of this book, but you should now have an idea of how rkt compares to Docker and how you can use it.

10.4 Summary

- Consider how logging fits into your workflow. What do you want the log data to provide?
- Backups can be expensive operations once your data grows, so plan accordingly.
- Plan your top-level scale vectors, and perhaps partition clusters using something like `role=highcpu`, for example.
- Keep an eye on rkt—it's going to continue to make waves.
- If you've reached the end of this book, don't forget to terminate your AWS instances.

index